Two Dc

Hugh Corcoran

LUNCHEON EDITIONS

Cover illustration by
Ildebrando Urbani
(Italy, 1946)

Two Dozen Eggs

POCKET STORIES FOR COOKS

Introduction by
Rachel Roddy

Illustrated by
Peter Doyle

Hugh Corcoran

LUNCHEON EDITIONS

'A chomharsnaigh chléibh, fliuchaigí mbur mbéal
Óir chan fhaigheann sibh braon i ndiaidh mbur mbáis.'

'Friends and neighbours, wet your mouths,
For after death you won't touch another drop.'

Cathal Buí Mac Giolla Ghunna
(Ulster, 18th century)

Contents

In ómós dó Rónán, a spreag mé ón tús.

And for my mother, Moya, who has
never ceased to encourage me in all my
endeavours, and who taught me to cook
and to love food and people.

An Introduction

I remember, very clearly, the first time I met Hugh. It was July, in the tree-lined piazza next to our block of flats in Rome. I wasn't holding a newspaper, rather the lead of our young black and white dog who provided an enthusiastic identifying feature, although I'm pretty certain we'd have recognised each other without her. Hugh was wearing a white shirt, half tucked into blue trousers, and carrying what seemed a small bag for someone who was travelling for a while. It turned out the bag also contained two bottles of good wine he'd carried from Paris, which, a few hours later, were sitting on my kitchen table.

Before the square and the table, we'd been corresponding for a year or so. Mostly practical things: the best pasta machine; a decent place to eat in Sicily; how thick we liked our pasta rolled. We'd also, thanks to the peculiarly intimate connector that is social media, seen enough glimpses of each other's tables and pans to know we liked cooking and eating the same things. And we were a professional cook and food writer: even if we didn't get on, we could surely talk about food. I often find myself apologising about our chaotic small flat, the streak of soot up the wall and dust on the shelves, but didn't on that particular occasion. It was a warm night and a mosquito coil burned. Vincenzo, my Sicilian partner, was around too so the three of us sat at the table, drank wine, ate bread, and then cooked, mostly vegetables, and appreciated Linton Kwesi Johnson's album *More Time*, although later I would discover that Hugh never listens to music when he cooks, but that's another story.

And we talked. Or maybe told each other stories is a better description And yes, I do feel pretentious putting it like that, but it's how things went. Stories about our childhoods in Belfast, Harpenden and a town in Sicily, youth clubs, teachers, pubs (lots of pubs), mothers, our first jobs, camping, train and bus journeys, stations, hotels, books, concerts, mistakes, moving around and staying in one place. We talked surprisingly little about food, although the stories were absolutely stuffed with it, with pans and pints and peelings. The Italian writer Italo Calvino said a good story can fill you almost as well as bread: that night we ate bread too so we were sated. It was so late it was early by the time we went to bed.

A few hours later we met up to drink coffee, then buy fish: monk, cuttle and gurnard from a stall that no longer exists on Testaccio market. Then later while Hugh made fish soup, he told me about a man from the Basque Country called Patxi who doesn't cut, rather cracks his potatoes apart with a little paring knife. It was then, standing near the stove with its headboard of soot, that Hugh first mentioned he had started to write short stories that might include *not recipes as such,* but short recipe notes. As the fish soup simmered in its wide, shallow pan and sent spits onto the white enamel, I told him I would like to read them.

Just over a year later I did. And a year after that they were bound into this book. Twenty-five windows into various lives. There is Patxi of course, who lives with Malen and was taught to crack potatoes by his mother.

Eneko has a restaurant near a river and never washes his cast iron pans. Then there is Sally Finnegan who lives on the sixth floor and is losing her eyesight; Brendan who rents a room from Mrs McGivern and thinks of the rain-drenched roads of the west of Ireland often; and young Fiontan Cassidy with his mop of blond hair eating a bacon sandwich into which his dad has carved the initials FC.

Twenty-five stories told in plainly beautiful language and brimming with everyday detail, human error, indulgence and humanity. They are not stories about food, but stories filled with food, both abundant and scarce, about kitchens, cooking and eating, both together and alone. It is not a recipe book, although out of every story comes a recipe – fish soup, Irish stew, roast chicken, kippers, lamb curry, orange cake. However, to list them like this does them a disservice: arrived at through the story, they feel essential, as do Hugh's wise and useful notes. Patience Gray believed good cooking is a mix of frugality and liberality. Hugh's cooking is exactly that, his story telling too, and it is a good thing both are bound in a book with such fitting drawings.

Sitting at my desk writing this, I can, if I look up, see the top of the kitchen dresser. I stand the empty bottles of wine I have enjoyed up there, like soldiers on the battlements of a castle. The two bottles Hugh brought from Paris in his bag are there of course, a dusty reminder of a good night and the start of a story.

RACHEL RODDY

ROME, OCTOBER 2023

Ticket Inspectors

The street lights lit the dark, empty streets as Inshaf sat inside the bus with his head resting upon the window and watched the stops pass, eagerly anticipating his own. He wore a baseball cap and his hand bore a plaster which he still had from when he cut his hand at the beginning of the week. He was on his way home after a long day. Every day was a long day for him. He began in the morning and left late at night. There was a break in between for a few hours but his house was so far away in the suburbs that there was no point in going home, and he thought he would be better spending the money on something else than travelling around in the metro. He had arrived in Paris just a few months ago and still didn't speak any French. He got by in English but each day was still a huge effort to learn everything he was taught in the kitchen and try to understand the French spoken all around him. A local girl, around his age, had offered to help him. He

sat with her most afternoons between shifts
and bought her a coffee in exchange for some
French lessons. She wore her hair short, with
a long fringe, she was in her early twenties,
pretty and curious about him. He accepted her
kindness and interest. Although he had been a
handsome young man to the girls back home,
no French women had shown any interest in
him until she had. So each afternoon he sat with
her and spoke about the most basic of French
vocabulary and, often, asked her would she like
to go out some time for a drink or dinner with
him, which she always bashfully declined. He
could never tell whether it was pity or attraction
which motivated her, he wasn't willing to probe
too much, for fear of losing her.

As he sat sleepily on the bus he imagined
his leg being warmed by a human hand, but it
was just the curry he had made for staff meal
and was bringing home for dinner. It had been
a long journey home. The metro had broken
down and everyone had been moved onto a bus
in that late hour and, not knowing French, he
had followed everyone towards the bus. The bus
pulled up at the next stop and two inspectors
boarded.

'Tickets please,' the inspector said impatiently.
Inshaf handed over his metro ticket casually.

'This is not a bus ticket.'

Inshaf didn't understand at first. He wondered
what the problem might be. He stood looking at

them in panic. A woman near him explained in English to him that he needed a bus ticket. He explained in turn, to the inspectors, although they made no sign as to the fact that they understood what he was saying, that the metro had broken down and that he was transferred onto the bus. They shook their heads when the translation came through.

'Fifty euros please.'

'Fifty euros? I can't pay fifty euros.'

'Fifty euros now, or you're off this bus.'

He sighed. It was late, almost one o'clock. He had work at nine the next morning. He looked at the woman who had interjected for help. She looked back apologetically. Just then a man interrupted from another seat.

'For god's sake leave him alone, he clearly didn't understand. We all just want to get home.'

'This is not your concern, sir,' said one inspector. 'Fifty euros! How would you like to pay?'

'I'm sorry, but this is so much money for me. It's a day's wages.'

'Cash or card, sir?'

'Cash.' Inshaf handed over the fifty euros from his wallet. He still wasn't working legally and was paid by the day. He had just been given it by the manager at the end of his shift. The inspector thanked him and placed the money in his wallet and moved on.

He hadn't understood, he explained again to the woman, but she was no longer interested.

It was over. He had lost his day's wages. He looked down at his curry. Lamb. He would at least enjoy that when he got back home. He began to do calculations in his head. How much will I earn if they take me every day for the next two weeks? Maybe I can stop the French lessons, then I won't have to buy the coffees. That will save me six euros per day. I'll have the fifty euros back in just over a week.

And so Inshaf rested his head back against the window and tried not to fall asleep and miss his stop again. And for the next week he cancelled his French lessons, but he was too ashamed to explain that he didn't have the money to pay for it, so he told her he had other things to do and the girl was hurt, he could see it in her eyes when he spoke to her in the café the next day. Then she laughed and explained that it was fine and that she also had plenty of other things to be getting on with and that maybe they should just leave the lessons altogether. He reluctantly agreed and that was the last day they met. He saw her, a few weeks later, smoking a cigarette outside a bar and kissing a boy; he put his hood up and quickly walked on, crossing the road so to avoid them. The rain had just started falling, the lights of the bar glowed orange and the couple were protected from the rain by the awning. He ran for cover, not wanting to get soaked on his way home, a man asked him for a lighter, he still didn't understand.

RECIPE

Lamb Curry

This is a Sri Lankan-style curry I learned from dishwashers and cooks I have worked with in Paris. Make a masala in a mortar and pestle with (all toasted) coriander, cumin, fennel seeds, fenugreek, cloves, cardamon and mustard seeds. Add fresh green chilli, ginger, garlic, turmeric and red chilli powder. Add salt and some neutral oil to loosen the mixture as you pound.

Rub this mixture on the lamb, either chopped into small or large pieces, or neck on the bone. Leave to marinate overnight in the fridge.

The following day let the lamb come to temperature by taking it out of the fridge some hours before cooking. Sauté some diced onions for around 30 minutes in ghee or sunflower oil. Then add the lamb and turn up the heat slightly. Add water, enough to just loosen a sauce which the meat can cook in without sticking, and reduce the heat.

To the sauce add lime leaves, a cinnamon stick, bay leaves and curry leaves. Simmer on a low heat until the lamb is tender.

Phone Calls from Leeds

Brendan stood in the hallway of Mrs McGivern's house, ringing in the numbers of his parents' telephone in Newport. He'd been living in Leeds for three years now and phoned home every week, sometimes more when he could buck up the courage to ask Mrs McGivern for another use of the telephone. The brothers and sisters had all contributed some money to buy a telephone for their parents back home so they could keep in touch as they all now lived in England, but most of them hardly ever called. They had moved on with their lives and settled in England now. The sisters went out with English men and gave their children English names, and they thought little of Newport. His two brothers hadn't been in touch in some time now. Manus, the eldest, was doing well and didn't bother much with Ireland. Danny, who was between the two, only contacted them to ask for money. Brendan had not forgotten, however, and after three years he still felt incredibly homesick at times. He pined for the country lanes and familiarity of the town and the people in it. He thought of the rain-drenched roads of the west of Ireland often, and the ferns, fuchsia and blackthorn wet with beads of fresh rain entangled with gates and stone walls. His street in Leeds seemed to him so plain and lacking in colour and texture. Even the red brick of the houses seemed grey on some days. He stood patiently as his mother's voice on the other side of the phone went through the daily motions of rural life. He listened to her and imagined where she was. The cottage, set in off the lane, protected by hawthorn and blackberry bushes. Her small garden which she tended and the turf shed which she made daily pilgrimages to, her journeys to mass every morning by foot and his father, cycling around the parish, delivering the post.

He spoke little of what he did. Mrs McGivern listened in to his conversations, he was sure, and he didn't want to share too much. Regardless, he didn't care to think of his life in England and only wanted to escape for half an hour each week and be transported back home.

Despite his pretence of being a rogue and his bravado in the bars of Leeds, singing and storytelling, he mostly felt depressed and alone in the city. He had not managed to meet any girls and he had taken up the habit of drinking much more than he used to in Ireland. The only person he'd had any interest in was a flamboyant young man he used to meet in a pub in London, but when his brother saw him he told him to stay away from the likes of him. Brendan knew what he meant. Most nights Brendan could be found in any one of several city centre pubs holding court and then singing his way home to sleep. He had worked on the roads and digging tunnels and now he was out of a job as he'd been thrown off a building site for trying to organise a union with some other men. There was a bundle of notes stuffed in his pocket which he was itching to spend on a new shirt and a few pints, but he was determined to keep it to pay the fare to London to see his sister and maybe get some work down there. He'd been told he'd have no bother finding it.

The voice of his mother told him goodbye and to take care and not get into any trouble and he quietly put down the receiver and placed a few pennies under the telephone for Mrs McGivern. Soon after, she poked her head through the hall doorway and asked if he'd like to stay for his tea. Mrs McGivern had been in England for forty years and she had never married or had children. She ran a little shop down the road which made repairs and alterations to clothes and curtains and the like. He didn't like to turn her down and he had little money to be feeding himself anyway so he accepted and sat at the kitchen table. The conversation was always quite serious and uninteresting to Brendan. Mrs McGivern was a very stern woman and had little to say for herself other than judging others around her.

She had wanted to be a nun in her youth but had
run away with a boy to England, who then broke
her heart and she never again showed interest in
men or romance or any of the light-hearted joys
of life. She believed in hard work and respectabil-
ity. She often thought poorly of Brendan but she
was nevertheless a kind woman and believed in
helping everyone.

Brendan wore a dark suit of tweed and a white
shirt which he had brought with him from
Ireland. He was still young but overweight and
bloated from the drinking and had bright
red cheeks and a mop of curly black hair. Mrs
McGivern sat him down at the table, draped with
a blue and white checkered oilcloth, and gave him
a plate of kippers and buttered bread. He poured
the tea and ate with great enthusiasm. When
finished, he offered to do the washing up, which
she declined as always, and so he said goodnight
and thank you and left to walk off into the
evening. It was not yet late and the birds were still
singing in the trees and the sun glowed orange
as it set in the distance. He walked slowly
with his head down, contemplating the things
his mother had told him. How she'd lost four
chickens to the fox and how the Lynches wanted
to sell the pub and move away. He thought again
of the sea and the gulls flying around the fishing
boats and the long, lonely walks around the bog
in Achill and how he'd sleep in the heather on
a summer's day after a morning of cutting turf

and a feed of sandwiches and milk. He took a left at the end of the street, turning towards the Bricklayer's Arms. Upon entering the busy room, he became a new man, as an actor might enter onto a stage.

RECIPE

Kippers

Kippers can be bought from a good fishmonger. They are extremely quick to prepare and can be kept for quite a long time. To cook kippers, simply poach for around two minutes in simmering water. Serve with butter, bread and a slice of lemon. A delicious tea for the family if you have nothing in. Also a treat on your own. Also a great birthday breakfast.

The Belles of Montmartre

The church bells could be heard loudly ringing from the Place des Abbesses to call the people to mass. The windows of Madame Montag's apartment lay wide open and the room was filled with sunlight, fresh air and the sounds from the square below. She had not been religious since she had first developed her critical faculties as a young girl. She had been born during the war into a communist family and had remained a member of the party throughout most of her life. Working as an historian, lecturing in the university and writing books in her spare time, she also sold the party newspaper on Sunday mornings until a few years ago. Now she left it to those younger than her to carry that banner but she still enjoyed chatting to them on her way back from shopping for the family lunch, her grandchildren stood around her, tugging at her coat sleeves and becoming anxious to go home, not interested in granny's opinions on imperialism. She had long, grey hair and wore thin, round spectacles and clothes that indicated that she cared little about her appearance. They were good clothes, but practical and often too big for her. She disliked anything too fitted or vain and preferred instead that jumpers and coats hung from her spidery figure. She rode a bicycle everywhere except when she was out walking and never learned to drive a car. She had travelled far in her younger days, to Eastern Europe and the Soviet Union, to Cuba and South America, to India and China but now in her old age she preferred not to leave her neighbourhood much and instead to entertain her family at home. From time to time she would telephone an old comrade and invite them over for a glass of wine and they would talk intensely about philosophy, history or political strategy for hours. She rarely talked about herself with her friends, almost never sharing her emotions or doubts or worries, finding that vulgar and far too personal for her tastes. She would instead hide behind what she saw as a higher form of conversation but one that never pushed her to open up to anyone else. Madame Montag had three grandchildren from her only daughter. She had been married to a theatre actor when she was younger for fifteen years but he had left her for a younger woman and dis-appeared from her life, only to come back when he was desperate and asking her for some money or a place to stay. Usually she would give in to him because she did not want her daughter to be ashamed of her father but she could not forget the months and years of heartache when she had been left alone with Rosa, her daughter, for a woman, a girl, ten years her junior.

The grandchildren ran around the modest apartment and helped their grandmother peel carrots, mix cakes and wash salads. They made a lot of noise which was a nice contrast to the lonely silence she experienced most nights. Although she put on a facade of wanting to be left in peace to read and think, she often felt lonely and appreciated the company and distraction of the children from time to time. Madame Montag brushed and washed the floors and told the children to lift their feet off the ground as she swept under them. The apartment was bright and airy and was lined with bookshelves containing books of all kinds: novels, encyclopaedias, history books, art books, photography and poetry. It was, however, except in the summer months, extremely cold as she refused to turn the heating on, saying that the simple solution to being cold was to put on another layer of clothing and she often slept in the month of December or January with a jumper and a woolly hat on her head. Today was warm and so she wore a large dress and an apron while she cooked. White beans stewed in a clay pot while she roasted lamb in the oven. She grated carrots for salad and asked the children to whip eggs for the orange cake, the oranges still boiling on the stovetop and giving off their bitter, floral perfume.

The children watched their grandmother
and repeated, a repetition from generation to
generation which echoed the repetitive manner
of kitchen labour; peeling, washing, whisking,
chopping, kneading. They had no idea who their
grandmother was other than being their grandmother, they hid underneath her large dress
and played with the tablecloth, using it to make
a tent where they pretended to be camping in
the wild. Their mother would arrive later. She too
had been let down by her partner, left to bring
up those children with her mother by a man
who had decided life was too short and moved
to America to follow his dreams. She spent the
morning buying flowers in the market and then
went to have a coffee with friends before lunch.
The women supported each other both because
of and in spite of their abandonment.

The sun disappeared behind a cloud and the
children asked their grandmother to close
the window for it was always cold in granny's
house. The closed room became filled with the
smell of roasting lamb, boiling oranges and
simmering onions, mixed with the smoke from
Madame Montag's cigarettes and the old smell
from the ancient books on the walls. Rosa came
back to find the children playing under a
tablecloth and her mother smoking on a chair
by the stove, reading a biography of the life and
times of Bertolt Brecht, a glass of wine in her
hand and a bottle open on the table. She kissed

her children, poured herself a glass of wine and set about setting the table while her mother laid the food upon it. As they sat around, her mother took each plate and placed a piece of sliced lamb and a spoon of beans upon it. The men in their lives were not missed, they ate and drank just as well without them, as did the children.

RECIPE

Carottes Râpées

To make a good carrot salad you must simply do one thing: never use a machine. Simply take the best carrots you can find, preferably directly from the earth, peel them and either cut them into very thin batons using a mandolin and a knife or grate them using a peculiar tool found in France which grates the carrot using a hand-turned mill. Next, season to taste with good-quality salt, black pepper, finely chopped parsley or chervil, lemon juice or red wine vinegar and high-quality olive oil, preferably not too young and pungent.

A Kitchen

Eneko ran a little restaurant on the banks of the River Bidasoa. 'Restaurant' is a grand word for what it was. It was a cabin surrounded by a small kitchen garden overlooking the river. Inside were three tables with benches against them, where people ate communally. His kitchen was open to the room, and consisted of a small gas stove, a heavy, stone sink, and an oven beneath the stove. Above hung the utensils and tools of the trade. Three large pots for stocks, deep and narrow; four to sauté and cook fish, absurdly wide and shallow; two cast-iron frying pans, never cleaned, for tortillas, salt cod omelettes, frying txistorra sausages and searing meat or frying eggs. A food mill, two of them in fact, a small one for the sauces and a big one for purées. A whisk for the mayonnaise, egg whites and cream. A set of knives sitting proudly on a magnet, serrated, big and small, heavy and light, sharp, pointed and broad, for slicing, mincing, sawing, snipping, clipping, chopping, boning, sowing and carving. The carbon steel was dull, but the knives deadly sharp and clean. Beside them on a bench, dusty

with flour, lay a jar full of wooden spoons, brush-
es, metal spoons, rolling pins, pastry palettes,
peelers and graters. Three mortars and their
pestles sat like Russian dolls, each their own size,
each for a different job, marble, wood and
terracotta. In the corner lay a collection of clay
pots of different shapes and sizes, some good for
stewing beans, others for stewing meat, some
empty with only the lingering smell of a winter's
stew, some full with vinegars and fermenting
vegetables and pickles. A basket of eggs, white
and brown and speckled, collected from the
chickens that morning sat upon a table and on
each of the other two, vases of flowers picked
from the garden. Upon the walls hung his onions,
garlic, rosemary, peppers, thyme, oregano, a
picture of Lenin and another of Argala. Upon
a heavy, olive wood chopping board sat a dead,
skinned rabbit and a cleaver. Onions were
stewing gently in a pot on the gas stove. A shelf
contained condiments and spices – paprika,
piquillo, mustard, coarse salt, fine salt, black
pepper, bay leaves, cayenne, confited garlic,
juniper berries, cloves, vinegars of cider, red wine,
white wine and sherry, olive oil, sunflower oil
and jars of cooking oil to be re-used. There were
also jars of tuna from the port at Ciboure,
dragged in by canes and hooks on the boats of
summer; anchovies from the Cantabrian sea
caught in their vast shoals by net and pulley;
guindillas, the little green peppers grown in his

garden and pickled in vinegar in the last days of summer; sardines from the Atlantic packed in oil; pâtés of duck and pork and chicken liver – from whenever they killed a pig or butchered a load of chickens and ducks and had to pluck the feathers in plastic bin bags; blood pudding from last winter's pig slaughter; fermented cheeses he'd bought on a trip to Catalunya; pickled vegetables a lady up the road brought him, cornichons, carrots and onions; and the rich, sweet foie gras of Jean Michel, his friend in Zuberoa.

The birdsong and river could be heard from inside the little cabin and that was the only music to be heard while he worked, cooked and served. Bottles of red and white wine, cider and Cognac were stacked against one wall and buckets of cold river water were taken in to chill them on warm summer days. A copper tap stood out from the wall where he continuously washed his hands, rinsed vegetables, cleaned blood from fish bellies, bathed lettuces and herbs, scrubbed pots and unmatching dishes which he'd found in the local markets. Small, unremark-able tumblers were stacked on a dresser which contained some plates, round and oval. The floor was stone and brushed regularly out the front door, into the garden. The chickens pecked at vegetable peels and loose flour which had fallen to the ground.

RECIPE

Rabbit

Rabbit is still eaten on a weekly basis by many families in Spain and France. I've had it most commonly in the Basque country, where housewives will cook it for Sunday lunch or workers will have it in a canteen on a Tuesday afternoon.

This is from my memories of a Sunday lunch in my old friend Arturo Villanueva's house. He was on the run at the time and his mother would come across the border to visit him, equipped with a rabbit stew.

A rabbit
A jar of piquillo peppers or several fresh ones
Olive oil
Garlic
Cayenne (whole)
Onion
Lardons, off-cuts of ham or chorizo
Smoked paprika
Bay leaves
White wine

Ask your butcher to cut the rabbit into small pieces. You can do this yourself with a good clever – I find the Chinese ones are best – but all the better if the butcher can save you the trouble. The leg, for example, should be cut into at least three pieces.

If you are using fresh piquillo peppers, it is important to roast them at a high temperature until blackened and remove the burnt skins, leaving only the flesh. Cut the peppers into strips.

Ideally use a wide, shallow sauté pan for this with a lid on it. Season the rabbit, fry it off and leave aside.

Add garlic, sliced, and a broken-up cayenne pepper to the pan. Once the garlic begins to brown, add a diced onion and some lardons. Cook this out for two minutes and add the sliced peppers, the paprika, the bay and deglaze with a dash of white wine. Cook together for around 15 minutes and then turn down to a slow simmer and add the rabbit. Cover and slowly cook the rabbit until tender, perhaps half an hour.

Good after a rest. Do not reheat the rabbit too aggressively.

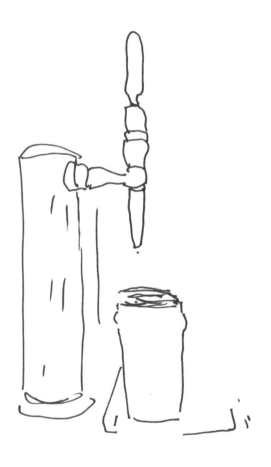

Eating Together

It was a bright and fairly warm Friday evening
when James McGahern strolled into town to
buy cigarettes along the country roads of County
Armagh. He was an older man and still a
bachelor. In his twenties he had gone to work in
England on the building sites and had spent his
time working and drinking and playing the fiddle
when asked to. He made little effort to find a
wife and was terribly shy of women anyway and
always had been. He was more interested in
pints of stout to kill the shyness he had in him and
this only led to loneliness and a drinking problem.
After many years away and having worked
all over England, finally settling in London, he
had decided to go home and take over the little
cottage where his parents had lived and which
he had inherited outside the village of Forkhill
under Slieve Gullion. He always wore a suit,
although he had only two, one for home and one
for the town. They were both quite worn and
shabby but the town one was made of nice
Donegal tweed and he was proud of it. He had

saved up his wages twenty years ago and bought it in a shop on Saville Row. He had found it hard to save and spent most of his meagre wages on rent, the pub and on a fry in the local café from time to time.

Since he had lived alone now for many years, he was used to it and had almost forgotten the loneliness he experienced when he first went to England and was instead timid now of human contact. As he walked into town on this lovely evening, he passed a woman on the way to the post office whose hair got stuck on his jacket. It had been blown wildly by the wind as they

crossed paths on the narrow footpath and had
wrapped itself around his lapel button. James
went red with embarrassment as the girl, shocked,
screamed and then, having realised what had
happened, began to attempt to unwind herself
from him.

The girl was only nineteen and her name was
Mairead Connolly. He knew her to see but had
never spoken a word to her. On many occasions
he had seen her coming out of the grocer's where
she worked and admired her young, good looks.
She often dressed in a short skirt and polished
leather shoes, her hair long and well brushed. He
had not lost all sexual desire but he never imagined himself with a woman anymore. He had been
with women in England, some English, more
Irish girls, and thought them foolish to have spent
the night with him, but not more than half a
dozen women in the lifetime he had spent over
the water, and since coming home he had barely
talked to a woman. When not at home, tinkering
around or watching the television or sometimes
playing the fiddle to amuse himself, he went
to the local public house to dull his boredom and
give himself something to help him fall asleep,
which is what drink had become to him. There
were never any women in the bar where he
always did his drinking. From time to time a man
might take his wife out for the night and they
would sit in the lounge, entered via another door.
And so most of his life was spent away from

their company, in the company of men of a similar
age to himself, and they rarely shared more than a
few distant words about the weather or politics
or the price of cattle.

As she untangled herself from his lapel, he
attempted to remove it in an effort to help her
but his movements only pulled at her hair which
seemed to give her a great fright so he stopped
altogether and stood there stupidly while she
worked it out. They then exchanged a few words
of apology and parted from one another, James
looking at the ground most of the time and then
heading straight to the post office to send a letter
to England and collect his pension. Mairead
headed in the other direction to the bank. She was
bringing money from the shop to the manager
there to put into their accounts.

After collecting his pension, he strolled across
the road to the grocer's where he met the young
girl once again. Shyly, he smiled at her and said
hello again. He was surprised to see her smile
back. He bought a packet of cigarettes, some soda
farls, half a dozen eggs, some sliced ham and
a pint of milk. That evening, after having made
his tea and settled into his armchair, he smiled
to himself about the funny events of the day,
and getting tangled in the young woman's hair.
He poured himself a glass of whiskey and fell
asleep on the chair.

Over the next six months, James would chat
to Mairead in the shop whenever he walked

into town. He always bought the same things, sometimes adding firelighters or bacon rashers or sausages. He rarely bought any vegetables, a rarity in the shop anyway, instead growing potatoes and cabbages at home which kept him going for the year. He had little curiosity to satisfy in the way of greens and fruits.

As the weather got worse coming into autumn, some days James would turn up to the shop soaking wet after having walked into town. Mairead asked him would he not take the car and he replied that he could not drive. He had never learned while in England or needed to. He had dug the London underground and then used it every day to get to work and the days when he didn't, he would be picked up on a corner by a van and driven to the site with a few other casual labourers. Mairead was shocked to hear he had no car but then wondered how he would run a car on such a low pension. He only ever bought the essentials to feed himself and saw a bar of chocolate as a once-a-week treat. She asked him would he ever be interested in coming over to her family home for Sunday lunch. At first he was embarrassed at the question, it sounded like something you would propose to a suitor, but soon realised that there was no way she saw him as a suitor, she was taking pity on him. He did not mind being taken pity upon, life had been so full of humiliations for James that he had little pride left. Poverty, a dependence on alcohol and his lack of love had left him at other people's mercy. He kindly accepted her offer.

On that first Sunday he felt ashamed of himself at the family table. They all dressed so well and looked so healthy. Mairead's brothers all played Gaelic football and they were all tall, well built, handsome men who sat up straight at the table and were always cleanly shaven. Her father was much the same, but older. He had also worked in England but had managed to save money and bought a bar. He didn't drink much himself but made a lot of money in the pub which James had known when he lived in Cricklewood. Mairead's mother had her good looks and always wore pearls and a nice dress on a Sunday; they were an impressive family to look at James thought. He sat in his best suit, wondering if he stank of cigarettes and drink and if he had shaved himself cleanly that morning, or if, as sometimes happened, he missed spots with his often-blunt razor. He rarely contributed to the conversation but once he had eaten and relaxed he would sometimes tell stories of where he had been and what he had done. Some were true stories and others were fabricated, patched together from bits and pieces of other people's lives and other men's fabricated stories. South Armagh at this time was a no-go zone for the British Army, they would have to move around in helicopters. Everyone was proud of the men who made it so, but when

James hinted that he might have been somehow involved, everyone knew that an old drunk had no place in the ranks of the local unit, but they smiled and nodded their heads to him.

They ate wonderful food at the house every Sunday. Sitting alone at night, he would look forward to the company and the pleasure of a good meal. He ate little when at home alone because he preferred to spend what little money he had on whiskey or beer but he enjoyed a big meal of roast meats and salads and pudding like Mairead and her mother would prepare. He noticed he had not the appetite of the men in the family who seemed to eat with no hope of ever being full, but he put away a second helping many times without hesitation.

Throughout the year he ate roast partridges, mutton pies, quiche Lorraine, watercress soup, liver and onions, spotted dog, ham hock salad, mussels, herrings and wild rabbit. His favourite was fish pie which he thought of as so satisfying and comforting and something he would never make himself. Watching the two women work in the kitchen, rolling pastry, washing salads, boiling potatoes and basting meat, he was always in awe of their mastery and skill. It was something he had never seen before or even considered a reality in Forkhill, but there were families who spent Sunday afternoons in this manner. Previous to falling into their company he would have spent Sunday afternoon reading the newspaper in the pub. He had stopped going to mass years before and now got up late and walked the country lanes and observed the wildflowers and birds until he arrived at the familiar door of the bar and went inside to sit and have four or five pints before heading home again along the lanes he came in by. His home was a small cottage sat against the hill, it was quite remote and at night he saw no lights from his home from neighbours' houses. The nearest was a fifteen-minute walk around the turn in the road. Trees sheltered the house from the harsh winds, but also made it dark and gloomy sometimes.

That winter, he spent his first Christmas in company in many years with the Connolly family. He stayed late into the evening, drinking whiskey, playing the fiddle and singing songs. Later, Mairead's father gave him a lift home. He said goodnight and went inside. That was the last thing James McGahern ever said to anyone. Some days later, he died in agony at home alone. He had liver cancer and hadn't told anyone. He had wanted to enjoy the time he had left with the Connollys and not upset them. He wasn't found until some days after he passed when he didn't turn up for lunch the next Sunday and no one had seen him about the town. Mairead and her father went to look for him at home and found the door unlocked and James lying in bed, the sheets unwashed and untidy. They gave him a wake in their home and the women cooked for all the neighbours who came to pay their respects. When they realised he had died penniless and without a family grave, they paid for the funeral costs and buried him with their own. Sunday lunches continued in the Connolly household, but they all talked about how they missed the stories, the music and the company of the old man who had spent his life alone.

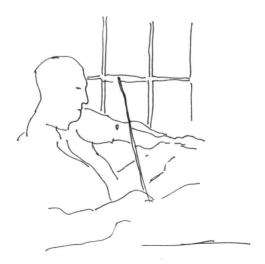

RECIPE

Fish Pie

Smoked haddock
White fish (hake, cod, whiting, monkfish or
  something similar)
Milk
Flour
Butter
Floury potatoes
Eggs

Poach the fish, half smoked haddock and half
white fish, in just enough milk to cover it.
Once cooked, set aside to cool and prepare a
roux with the flour and butter. Slowly add
the poaching milk and make a thick bechamel.
Meanwhile, boil the peeled potatoes and
strain, allowing them to steam for a while in
the pot.

Mash the potatoes, adding plenty of butter.
Flake apart the poached fish and place in a
baking tray, pouring over the bechamel. Boil
some eggs for six to seven minutes and
carefully peel them; they should be soft boiled.
Place them with the fish, sliced in half, and
spread the mashed potato on top. Mark lines
and ridges across the mashed potato; these will

go crispy when baking later. Heat the oven to 200°C and bake until there is a nice browning on top of the pie.

Serve with a fresh green salad, ideally of edible garden leaves such as watercress, rocket, dandelion, pennywort, tansy, fat hen or sorrel.

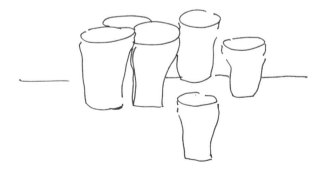

Many Cooks

On a bench sitting outside a building, some miles beyond the village of Besalú in the Catalan province of Girona, three men sat in the sun. They were not looking at one another but all facing into the horizon. The farmhouse stood on a hill which overlooked the plains below and, later, out to the Mediterranean sea.

The men were dressed in simple dark suits of cotton, which looked hot in the afternoon sun. They wore caps which shaded their faces from the sun and two of the men had moustaches, the other a huge beard. They were not dress suits but working clothes. The jackets railwaymen once wore, or, in this case, poor peasants who had bought them in town many years previously. The men were shepherds, but they were getting old and didn't like to walk too far nowadays. Instead, they preferred to meet up and smoke cigarettes and drink wine and cook together while their sheep ran almost wild and ate the sweet mountain herbs which grew in the dry tundra. Only the dogs cared now where the sheep went.

The house behind them was a simple and small dwelling. It was, in fact, a mountain refuge for shepherds, one that they had built themselves in their youth. It consisted of a small room flanked by wooden bunk beds built into the walls and at the end of the room a small wood-burning stove used for heating and cooking. There were no windows in the dwelling. Outside, some terracotta pots, some broken, some not, lay around filled with useful herbs for cooking and peppers which, when harvested, were dried out and left to hang in the sun.

The men's faces had the appearance of tanned leather as they smoked rolled cigarettes and sipped red wine in silence.

From within, a smell of cooking was wafting into the hillside around them. A smell that mixed with tobacco smoke, wild savoury and thyme and the beastly smell of half-wild sheep. They had spent a day, a week previous to now, hunting snails in the shrubbery and rocks of the hillside. They had been doing it since they were boys and it did not take long to find them, they knew well where to go. Then, they tied them in a net and left it hanging in the refuge, purging them. When three days had passed they gathered mountain herbs and had taken some grain from the town and brought it to feed the snails. For three more days the snails feasted on wild mountain herbs and became fat. This morning, they had arrived to the little crate used as a cage for the snails to find them fat and healthy. They lit a fire and brought some water to the boil, meanwhile washing the snails with vinegar and water. Next, they boiled the snails and rinsed them. The sauce was made and was slowly cooking on the stove inside. The inside of the building was much too hot now in the midday heat with the stove lit to spend more than a few minutes in. The men were outside under the shade of a tree smoking and pulling snails from their shells with their wives' hairpins and flicking the meat into a large ceramic bowl in front of them which was decorated with paintings of flowers and plants.

The men took off their working jackets and rolled up their sleeves as they picked through the snails. One stood up to check the sauce. He approached the pot and tasted it with a wooden spoon. Reaching above the stove he plucked a dried chilli pepper from a string and crumbled it into the sauce. His bones were stiff and sore, and he found it hard to stand up and sit down these days. He turned around and went back towards his dining partners. A dog came running enthusiastically towards him looking for attention, he petted its head and ushered it away.

In the distance he could see the front. The Franquistas were approaching fast; he knew the Republican forces would not hold them off, he had asked a young girl in the town to read the newspaper to him and each week the front was retreating backwards. A young Polish man had come to the village a week ago; he had crossed the Pyrenees on foot and was looking for the front. He had told him to go back and not be so silly as to get himself killed for a lost cause. These were the last days of the war and everyone knew it. The young man was a trade union organiser and had come all the way from Warsaw to help and was not willing to turn back now. He promised to keep in touch as he marched on towards the bombing, a pathetic rifle hanging over his shoulder. He didn't expect to hear again from the boy.

The men finished their work and one of them brought the large terracotta pot out from the stove and they mixed in the snails. One by one they laboriously stuffed the snails in their sauce back into the shells. This was long work, but they had little to eat and almost nothing else to do. The pot went back to the stove then and they poured some more wine.

A child came from the village in a great hurry. She ran to the men as if her life depended on it. The war, it was over, the Republic had surrendered.

The men invited the young girl to eat with them. They set up a table in the dry ground under a tree and threw a checkered cloth over it. They all began to eat with their hands from the great terracotta pot, sucking the sauce and snails out, which stained their moustaches and beards in red sauce. The young girl looked on excitedly and ate with relish. The sheep chewed the shrubs as usual and the dogs barked and played.

RECIPE

Cargols a la Llauna, or Snails in the Catalan Style

If you collect your own snails from the wild they need to be purged in a similar way to that explained in the story. If you buy fresh farmed snails or frozen, there is no need for this process. Setting up a little snail farm in the garden is quite an interesting pursuit, however, if you have the means and the time.

Lardons or off-cuts of jamon
Olive oil or lard
Garlic
Onions
Tomato conserve
Paprika
Dried chilli
Savoury
Laurel
Thyme
Boiled snails

Cook the lardons or jamon, cut into small pieces, in some olive oil or lard. Add garlic and cook until almost brown. Next add an onion or two finely diced and lower the heat, cooking the onion until soft and translucent; this should take around 30 minutes. Next add the tomato conserve, only a little to loosen the sauce, either whole peeled tomatoes or passata. And then the herbs and spices along with a little glass of water and season with salt. Let it cook out for an hour. You can adjust the seasoning with vinegar too.

Once the sauce is cooked, the boiled snails should be pulled from their shells, the black bit at the end removed, and then mixed in the sauce and replaced in the shells. This seems like a lot of work, but it is worth it. Reheat (this can be done a day in advance) and serve to guests willing to suck out the insides and get their hands dirty. You may need to serve toothpicks or long utensils used for eating crab.

Midnight Snacks

In October, the colour of the leaves began to
change on the trees from green into yellow
and the rain, relentless in that town as it was,
washed them into the drains and gutters which
lay blocked with an array of autumn. The cold
had not properly set in yet, but Peadar wore
a raincoat most days and his woollen jumper to
keep the chill off of him. He walked down by
Stephan's Green with his flute under his right
arm, wrapped up in a newspaper. The light was
fading now come seven or so and the air fresh
and biting. He hurried into Mulligan's public
house and stood at the bar, ordering a pint of stout
and keeping his flute tightly wrapped under
his arm. Quietly and discreetly, he watched the
musicians and listened to their lively notes.
The bar was dark inside and he could see the
street lights coming on outside. He calmly
supped his pint and sunk into the atmosphere,
peace in a warm little oasis, an escape from his
damp, lonely house. After drinking half the
pint he could feel his nerves relaxing and his
head getting slightly lighter, the weight on his

shoulders lessen. He greedily poured the rest of it back down his neck.

The barman looked at him as if to signal for another.

'A bird never flew on one wing,' he chimed.

A whiskey on the side, one of those from the north, cuts the back of your throat, somewhere between Scotland and here. Dal Riada, now that's a place. He drank the strong, dark whiskey and helped the blow of it by chasing it down with another mouthful of stout. The stool beside him now looked necessary. He put his money on the counter and left it there, in a neat pile beside his pint. The barman reached into it and took out what he needed. From the crowd of musicians a man came to ask him to play a tune. He wasn't thinking of joining them, but sure since they asked. He unwrapped his newspaper to reveal his Hammy Hamilton flute, a northerner also, he finished his whiskey and blew a note. As he blew, brown stout dripped from his moustache onto the black wood of the flute. One, two notes, and he's off. A lively reel, *The Limerick Lassies*, gets people on their feet in the country, but these Dubliners rarely dance, they just tap their feet and listen.

He closed his eyes and blew rhythmically and steadily into the instrument, his fingers beating off the holes. In the midst of his blindness, he could hear dancing beyond his playing. Through the notes he heard what he remembered to be feet beating on the floorboards. He opened his eyes and watched a girl in a long skirt dancing in front of him. She danced a reel in the old way on her own, but then her dancing became more sensual, she left the tap-dancing and began to move her hips back and forth and from left to right. She looked at him dead straight in the eye and followed every note. When he played he felt her body move to it, in one moment he imagined they were joined together. When he stopped there was an applause from those around and he took a breath for air and then went back to his pint, barely looking at her. It was her who came to him, full of confidence and curiosity, nothing that he was used to. There they talked for a long time, Peadar calling for rounds like he didn't have rent to pay next week. She was from the Gaeltacht of Kerry, but her mother was Italian, she named her Chiara. She was much slimmer and smaller than him, but she spoke much more surely of herself and steered the conversation any way she wanted; he gladly followed.

He had not had a summer love, which everyone talked of. He had spent it alone and sometimes looking at girls from afar. He spoke no Irish but he wanted to learn every language she knew and speak it with her. He wished to forget English and only speak Italian and Gaelic to her and mix the poetry and love language of both those tongues. She spoke energetically and honestly to him and he wanted to hear everything. They played again, three Kerry polkas, and this time she played the box as he, for the first time, led. After, they ordered two more whiskeys for the road and gently packed away their instruments. He thought of his lonely, cold house, the mess of the half-eaten takeaway on the table and the cigarettes still in the ashtray. How he'd never gotten around to decorating the place and how even if it wasn't cold, it would still feel cold to her. They walked to her house without asking. She invited him in and asked had he eaten dinner. She made him spaghetti in tomato sauce and opened a bottle of red wine. They sat up and played for each other, with each other, until the early hours of the morning before she invited him to share her bed.

In the morning the rain teemed down upon the sodden yellow leaves and the wind rattled the window as he watched her sleeping body in the light of the undrawn curtains. He could see a neighbour cleaning leaves off the front of his car and an old woman carrying shopping precariously down the road. In the corner of the room lay their instruments, unprotected now outside their cases, his newspaper thrown to one side. She breathed heavily and turned in the bed, he went back to her and closed his eyes, to become blind once again.

RECIPE

Spaghetti in Tomato Sauce

Bring some water to a rolling boil, salted generously with good sea salt (*gros sel* in France) and add your pasta.

Meanwhile, thinly chop some garlic, to your taste, and fry in olive oil. Add tomato passata or peeled tinned tomatoes, or alternatively fresh when in season and good. Season with salt, peperoncino, sugar and vinegar. You may also add some basil, oregano or anchovies.

Once the pasta is cooked, toss it in the sauce and serve with or without Parmesan or pecorino.

A Painful Lunch

A ginger cat slept lazily on the wall separating
Monsieur Le Clerc's garden from his neighbour's.
The garden boasted trellises of roses and large
terracotta pots full of hydrangea, lavender and
peonies. He sat at a wrought iron table smoking
a cigarette peacefully in the sun, his glass half
empty, smells of a poaching chicken coming
from the kitchen where his wife was at work.
Monsieur Le Clerc was very satisfied with himself,
satisfied with his lot, which he had made, in his
own eyes. He looked around him at the house
and garden which he had inherited from his
poor, darling mother and closed his eyes to enjoy
the warmth of the late morning sun. Madame
Le Clerc had invited some friends for lunch, a
young couple she had been introduced to in the
market who had just opened a little restaurant
in the neighbourhood. As he relaxed into the
heat and began to drift off he heard excited
voices, greeting and exchanging remarks, and
then his wife call him to meet the guests. They
went to him in the garden and, upon realising that
he must rise to kiss them both, he gently lifted

himself out of his seat and casually embraced the two.

'This is Marie and Vincent,' announced his wife. Monsieur Le Clerc smiled vaguely at the both of them. 'They have just opened a restaurant ten minutes from here.'

His vague smile sat disinterestedly on his face and he poured himself another glass of wine. 'They've brought you some wine,' his wife said finally.

He took the bottle, examined it, put it back on the table and sat down again in his seat. Monsieur Le Clerc saw no reason to show any sign of enthusiasm or interest in other people or what they had achieved or what their various opinions were. In fact, he thought it vulgar to do so. In his opinion, even too much of a smile was a sign of stupidity and weakness and for that he hated his stupid, vulgar wife for her curiosity in others. Her enthusiasm about this couple embarrassed him, and was a disgrace to his standing in the community in which they lived.

'Do you know the wine?' asked the young woman. 'I hear you are a great connoisseur of wines,' she added, flatteringly.

He looked at her with the same disdain he had for his wife when she tried to flatter him, but with a little more attention as Marie was thirty years younger than his wife and wore a well-fitted summer dress which showed off her young breasts and soft, unblemished skin.

'I don't, no,' he replied quietly and turned to read the newspaper he had been studying before he had been interrupted by the company.

Marie bowed her head as her husband stood politely nearby, not speaking. Madame Le Clerc announced that she would bring some glasses of Champagne to begin the afternoon. The couple stood and watched Monsieur Le Clerc read his newspaper in silence and awkwardly looked at one another. Before arriving, their chatter had been lively on the way down the street as they strolled and held hands. Now, embarrassed and ashamed, they stood apart and waited for a response from Monsieur Le Clerc which never came and were only relieved by Madame Le Clerc's arrival with the Champagne glasses. They gently clinked glasses and looked at each other intensely, as is customary in France, as they drank a toast to friendship.

The conversation turned to lunch and comments were made about the wonderful smells coming from the kitchen.

'Well, my wife is a wonderful cook,' Monsieur explained. 'We eat extremely well in this house. Almost every day in fact. It's very important for us. We take food very seriously here. He who doesn't take his food seriously, doesn't take himself seriously.' He smiled at both of them.

'And that would be a great mistake!' his wife joked. He did not see the joke. Feeling somewhat put out by the joking, he excused himself and went to the bathroom. There he pissed into the bowl and wondered whether the young woman might be impressed by him. He was not what he was in his youth, that was for sure, but he was confident he still had it in him. He thought he'd caught her admiring him, a touch of desire in her stare. He zipped himself up and moved to wash his hands. Looking into the mirror, he combed back his black hair which covered the balding spot on the crown of his head. When he rejoined the company, they had moved inside to sit at the dining table in the large kitchen. He arranged the couple's wine at the back of a cupboard and reached for some bottles which he liked to drink on a daily basis. He opened one and explained that this was a very, very excellent wine and left them in no doubt as to how lucky they were to be drinking it.

Lunch was poached chicken and vegetables. He relished it and congratulated his wife on yet another perfectly cooked meal. As the lunch wore on, conversation becoming less and less attainable, the subject came up of an excellent tagine restaurant around the corner.

'I don't care for that myself, just throwing spices around, no finesse. I enjoy the purity of flavour in the French table. Good old-fashioned French cooking, like that of my youth and my mother. None of that nonsense indeed. Aromatic my eye! How about masking rotten meat! That's what it's about. Now, something so simple and elegant as a poached chicken, that's cooking,' he announced definitively. Everyone at the table listened and nodded in agreement. It was just then that Monsieur Le Clerc began to choke on a piece of dry chicken breast he had been having difficulty swallowing. They all sat staring at him, unsure whether to make a fuss or not. They certainly did not want to appear to be hysterical. After a moment he fell sidewards from his chair and his wife put her napkin upon the table and ran over to help him. She asked the couple to help her or phone an ambulance, but within a few minutes he had managed to cough up the dry chicken breast and catch his breath again. Mortified by his mistake, he excused himself and left the room. His wife followed him out and then announced that he had gone to lie down and that she would promptly serve dessert. The old man slept soundly on his own in the next room and, after having eaten dessert and drank coffee with Madame Le Clerc, the couple left, thanking her for their hospitality and good company and promising to come back soon.

RECIPE

Poached Chicken

Take a young chicken, the best you can find, but preferably one of those yellow, French birds, raised in the open air, and truss it. Cover with water, adding an appropriate amount of salt, and some seasonal vegetables. My favourite time to prepare this dish is in spring and include peas, young carrots, an artichoke heart or two, broad beans, a little leek and young onions. Turnips are a fine addition too.

Bring it to the boil, an oval Le Creuset pot is best, and turn down to a simmer. Simmer for around 45 minutes to an hour. It should ideally be just cooked, not falling apart, to prevent the breast from becoming dry. Season with plenty of black pepper. Mustard, mayonnaise or aioli is a good accompaniment, but equally it is perfection alone with a bottle of chilled, light red wine.

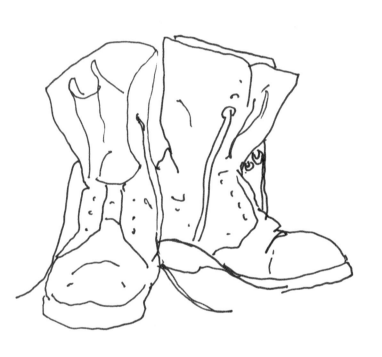

Last Night's Fun

A dull morning light lit the kitchen in the back
of Donal Mac Fheidhlimidh's bungalow,
or rather his mother's bungalow, in the fields
beyond Hilltown, County Down. Donal sat with
his head resting upon one hand, slowly eating
his breakfast with a fork in the other. It was
a good breakfast of high-quality rashers and
sausages from the man up the road and some
eggs from his mother's chickens. She had even
gone to the trouble of making potato bread
with last night's mash and buying in black
pudding. Donal wore loose-fitting trousers and
no shoes and the same white shirt he had
been out in the night before and had also slept
in. It was stained down the front with splashes
of brown porter which he had not noticed in
the excitement of the evening. He'd spent it in
Madden's Bar in Belfast, only getting home in
the very late hours of the morning after a long,
winding drive through the County Down
countryside during which he sat swaying in the
back of the car and had to ask his compatriots
to pull over for a minute while he threw out

the night's refreshments along with the rest of his stomach.

His mother sat across the table from him, nicely dressed in a flowery blouse and long skirt, staring at him while she drank her tea.

'Are you going to look for some work today, Donal?' she asked him.

'I am, of course,' he replied lazily without looking up.

'You will in your...!' She stopped and put the tea on the table. 'What in God's name did you get up to in Belfast yesterday? You told me you were going to the Linen Hall Library to borrow a book on the Annals of the Four Masters and you come back at God-knows-what-hour and woke the whole house up with your tripping up the stairs and making a mess in the toilet.'

'Aw, would ya leave me in peace. I was only going to get a book, sure, and I missed the last bus home because the Orange Men had blocked the road.' Donal groaned into his plate.

The rashers were indeed excellent. He cut them with his knife and made a little pile on his fork of rasher, sausage, egg and potato bread and stuck it in his mouth, washing it down with hot tea. The tea is always hot here, he thought to himself warmly. His brown suede jacket hung over the empty chair beside him where he had left it last night, or early this morning. It contained a copy of *An Béal Bocht* in one pocket, a crumpled up ten pound note in the other and

a tin whistle in the inside pocket. He remembered back to the night previous and thought
of the music flowing in the pleasantly lit bar.

He'd sat at a table, receiving pint after pint
of brown stout and drinking them back with
great ease as he played tune upon tune on his
whistle to the great amusement and celebration
of the crowd around him. He had met some
country men that afternoon while walking
through Belfast who had offered him to join
them in a licensed premises for a jar or two. He
couldn't see the harm in that anyway. The men
were great musicians from County Armagh and
brought songs and poetry with them too. His
mother had warned him about keeping bad
company, but good company was his downfall.
The conversation flowed and songs were sang
and tunes played and dances danced and before
he was aware of the time or had thought to
look at his watch it was nine in the evening and
the last bus to Hilltown had departed from the
Europa Bus Centre.

He remembered meeting a Belfast man who
asked what he was reading. The man was both
greatly surprised and impressed to hear it was in
the Irish language. A look of deep interest came
over his face as if he was meeting a very foreign
and exotic type from a faraway continent, or
perhaps from another time. When asked what
he did, Donal replied that he liked to play the
whistle, drink stout, read, go for long, rambling

walks, write poems and spend long hours debating with friends in public houses. No, what do you do for a job, the man meant, still looking at him like he was a lunatic.

'Oh,' said Donal, 'I don't. I'm on the dole since I left university in Galway and I like to read in bed most of the day and then maybe have a pint in the evenings, I don't know how I could fit in any time for work.'

The tea was now at the perfect temperature and was quenching his terrible thirst and helping his headache. As was the greasy, heavy breakfast filling his emptied stomach.

'So where is the book you borrowed?' asked his mother.

Donal glanced around the room and at his jacket pocket innocently.

'I must have left it at the library. Don't I have terrible luck! I was so worried about missing my bus,' Donal lied. 'You couldn't lend us a tenner to get the bus back up today and see if it's still there?'

RECIPE

Ulster Fry

An Ulster fry differs from a fry in the rest of
Ireland because of its inclusion of soda and
potato bread. In the south they tend to just serve
toast, a sad and miserly option. Apart from
that it consists of sausages, bacon, black
pudding, white pudding and eggs. The bacon
should be good and fatty, preferably bought
from a good pig farmer who breeds healthy
animals, full of fat and tasty meat. Anything
else defeats the point and most of Ireland now
is addicted to very sad and dull breakfasts
which have become the culture there.
Things such as Denny's sausages, which Irish
immigrants in England will search out. Absolute
rubbish. A generation ago those things that
pass for sausages now would have been shunned.

This is the consequence of the supermarket generation. Better to support a good local farmer, rather than imported Danish industrial pork.

You can make your own sausages, or source them from a good artisan butcher. Curing your own bacon is easy. Just rub equal amounts of salt and sugar on a pork belly for five days, changing the container and cure each day, and then hang it for a week or so and you'll have something you can slice and fry up for breakfast. A good egg is also a fine thing if there ever was one, as fine as anything. An egg on its own would be enough and as good a breakfast as on any table in Ireland. But try to find someone who can sell you good eggs, or get a few chickens if you have enough space.

Potato bread is made with leftover mash. Mix flour into it until you have a workable, doughy mixture and add a little pinch of baking powder. Roll thin and cook on a dry pan. Soda bread is mentioned elsewhere in the book and is extremely easy to make.

Large pots of steaming tea are traditionally served with an Ulster fry.

A Satisfying Meal

Camille was always regarded with some suspicion among her colleagues. She worked as a dishwasher in a small yet highly pretentious restaurant in the French countryside. No one could understand, particularly between these highly ambitious cooks and waiters, why a woman of forty-odd years was still working as a dishwasher. Some said she was a drug user because of her marked face. She was missing some teeth and her cheeks were hollowed in. It was true she could well have been a heroin addict from the look of her. However, the real reason was that she had not worked for the last twenty years since she had had children and now that she had divorced her husband and the children had left home, she was forced to find employment as she had no other income with which to pay the rent. Because, of course, she was never financially compensated for looking after the children for twenty-odd years. Her face was worn and teeth were missing because she ate badly and smoked too much. She had lost a tooth once when her husband hit her after a night in the pub but she was never gifted with beauty from the beginning. Night and day she scrubbed pans, rinsed plates and threw out bin bags, which did not make her look any more attractive. Over the months and years, she began to neglect her appearance, as no one ever commented upon it anyway, and on her days off, tired and lonely, she would eat crisps and smoke cigarettes and sit in her pyjamas, bored out of her mind. The job did not pay enough to allow her to go to restaurants or to hang around bars trying to meet new partners. Even had it done, there was nowhere to go in that miserable little French village where she lived. It had no bar, no café and the only restaurant was the one she worked in. She had moved from one miserable provincial town to an even sadder provincial village. Originally they had moved because her husband had found work there with a winemaker in one of those big, commercial wineries which employ immigrant labour from Eastern Europe. Her husband wasn't Eastern European, but he had trouble finding and keeping work and, because no one else wanted to do it, it was easy to find work labouring on those big monocultures of Chardonnay and Pinot Noir.

From time to time, she ate a little better at the restaurant. Almost never at a table though, usually she ate like a frightened mouse, nibbling hungrily and then looking up to see if she was being watched. She ate in the corner of the dishwashing pit off a shelf. When she was given food, in the same way as a prisoner or hostage is passed food into their cell, she took it greedily and placed it on the shelf above her work station. When there were no plates to wash or onions to peel she would return to her stored food, as a squirrel might, and stuffed some into her mouth. Pieces of roast duck, offcuts of cake, some discarded vegetables, a little cold broth, a piece of cheese on bread. The cook who fed her did so out of generosity and kindness. He too ate like that, albeit from his own cooking. The owner never bothered to ask if anyone had eaten or not and of course the answer was usually not. The owner, a proud man from a bourgeois background who had fallen upon some inheritance and came out to the countryside to buy his dream restaurant in the heart of the wine-making region, was quite embarrassed about how badly his staff lived. He knew they were badly paid and never took breaks, never ate well and worked many more hours than were in their contracts, but at heart he was a coward and he dared not to ask questions of all this. He accepted it as the only way to do things and didn't see himself or anyone else capable of changing it. He enjoyed his leisurely lifestyle, coming in from time to time to have lunch or lecture the staff on his latest musings about which direction the restaurant should take and he took great self-importance from this. He liked to think that he had changed

the town, the region even, with his wonderful
restaurant. He saw himself as a sort of renaissance
man, a man of culture and art who appreciated
the finer things in life, good produce and fine
wines. The fact that most of the produce his
cooks used was not particularly good did not
bother him because he did not ask as long as the
money was coming in, and in truth he did not
know the difference between a good lettuce and
a bad one, despite hoping that he would. One
day, when the waiter had drunk the last bottle
of a rare wine while drunk after work one night,
he had asked to be served that very bottle from
the cellar. The waiter, guessing he may not know
the difference, had simply poured an old plonk
into the nice bottle and served it at the table.
His boss declared it a piece of mastery, although
perhaps not showing as well as it could have.

Camille was scrubbing a pot which had been
burned to black and needed a steel wool brush
and a spoon to remove the burned sauce at the
bottom when she was interrupted by the cook
and asked if she'd like to eat. She replied that
she would; it was three o'clock in the afternoon
and she had only had a coffee and a cigarette
since she woke up at seven. He told her that they
would eat at a table after lunch service was over.
Sometimes when he was ahead of his work or
had something good to share he proposed
that they eat at the table after the service was
finished. This was rare as he was usually too busy

but today there must have been something to share. Camille put her head down again and scrubbed pots and dishes until the last customer left. Then, smelling the intoxicating aroma of roasting fat which was being prepared for her, she left her dishcloths and apron aside and went to the kitchen to watch. There he was, in his dirty white jacket and apron, stirring mashed potato in a copper pot and opening and closing the oven to check the progress of his caillettes ardèchoises, chard and pork faggots from the Ardèche region where he was from. These were never on the menu, the owner thought of them as far too provincial and brutish to be served to paying customers, but they reminded the man of home and he made them from time to time with the leftover scraps of pork he cut from the bones of more noble cuts.

She went and set a table and asked the waiter if he was eating with them. He replied that he wouldn't, as expected. He was a pretentious little git who never saw the value in peasant cooking and disliked the meals proposed by the cook. He agreed on many points with the owner and liked to do exercise after service, taking pride in his figure, going for a run or to lift weights at the gym rather than eat fatty faggots and drink wine in an empty restaurant like the fat cook he secretly despised.

Together, the two of them sat there, tucking into the caillettes without talking. They drank a glass of wine to appreciate the meal. After, they smoked a cigarette in silence like lovers just after a fit of desire. Camille put out her cigarette and, like a woman rising from bed to put on her dressing gown, wrapped her apron around her and tied it around her waist, moving off to the dishpit, tying her hair back into a bun.

RECIPE

Caillettes Ardèchoises

To prepare the caillettes you will need plenty of chard leaves or spinach, minced pork and perhaps a little liver in there too. You will also need, importantly, to get your hands on some caul fat.

Wash the leaves thoroughly and blanch them in salted water, squeeze out any water and leave to cool.

Meanwhile, prepare the meat by seasoning with salt and pepper and a little nutmeg if you like. Add an egg per kilo of farce, a little stale bread first soaked in water and then squeezed, and a little garlic too.

Once you add the greens you should have quite a green stuffing for the caillettes. Make them into balls around the size of a tennis ball or smaller and wrap them in a layer or two of caul fat. Place them into an oven tray with stock or water to cover half, and cover with tin foil or a lid. Cook on a medium to low heat for around two hours.

Excellent served with mashed potatoes or, better yet, celeriac and potato mash. Also good served with a little salad such as lamb's lettuce and some mustard on the side.

Swimming

The day was already warm by the time Ana had woken, dressed in her labouring clothes and went out of the house into the sunlit yard, basking in the orange light of the early morning, crossed it and entered the barn to feed the sheep.

She had dark hair which fell upon her thin, freckled face and a slight figure. Sometimes it appeared uncanny when she performed her jobs on the farm, usually reserved for men twice her size, and yet she carried them out with ease most of the time.

She had awoken at sunrise as was her habit now and went to do her morning work before preparing lunch for some visitors who were arriving later that afternoon. At times she resented the extra work laid down by these town people who came expecting to be well fed and with glasses never empty but who offered little in the way of help and brought such meagre gifts as was laughable to her. Nonetheless, she looked forward to the afternoon's event as it was a break from the sometimes lonely and monotonous

labour of the farm. Ana had never met anyone
and never married. Her interests were not in men
and she had always enjoyed work and leisure
alone but this did not keep her from feeling from
time to time that she lacked company in life.

She had slaughtered two lambs the day before
and hung them in her own barn. She would now
light the fire which would later serve to roast
the lamb and tie the carcasses with metal wire
to a spit. The morning was calm and the sounds
of cars upon the road nearest the house had not
yet begun. Only the sounds of the sheep and
lambs within the barns, the chickens pecking and
rooster crowing, the wild birds singing upon
the trees and her dog running around her feet.
She tended to the sheep and checked them as
she often did throughout her day to make sure
they were all alive and well. Soon she would
milk them and begin the process of making her
cheeses, but first she would sit down to
breakfast and think over the day ahead. She sat
inside the dark kitchen at her sturdy wooden
table and stirred hot milk into her coffee. She
ate yesterday's old bread with some cheese and
a boiled egg, taken from the coop on the way
to the kitchen. Frying the bread in some pork fat,
she thinly sliced some tomme and placed it on
the plate with the soft-boiled egg. This would
be her calmest moment in the day, the rest
would be dedicated to work and hosting. She
savoured it, knowing the way ahead.

As the morning sun rose over the small farm-
yard, the fire of wooden logs slowly burned
down to hot cinders and the lamb was erected
over them and left to cook in the heat. Turning,
from time to time, with the help of someone's
hand. She went to the garden to collect some
salads, leaves and flowers which she brought into
the kitchen and washed in the old marble sink
which served to wash vegetables, plates and pots
alike and often the soiled hands of farm labour.

By this time Ana's mother, Marie, had arrived
to help set the table for lunch. A big stout woman,
she was at least three times the size of her
daughter and almost the same height, which
was not very tall. She wore a large, flowery dress
and an apron over it almost all day. Her hair
was cropped short, and she wore glasses when
reading or doing more delicate work in the house.
A trestle table was set out under the climbing
vines in the yard where a little shade was given
by the leaves and the trees surrounding it. An
embroidered, white cloth was thrown over the
wooden boards and she went to pick wildflowers
to put into water glasses to decorate the table.
The plates arranged upon the table were not
delicate and were of the practical type you may
find in any country inn or canteen and of a
white dulled by years of use.

Marie's husband had died the previous year and
she felt his absence painfully on days like these.
He was a man of great character and would have

held court, telling jokes and stories at the table and pouring cider until evening. Last year they had held a similar lunch and afterwards they had all gone to the river to cool off. Jean-Michel, her husband, had never swam before, he was seventy-four years old. Those from the town asked in amazement had he never been to the seaside. Once, he told them, as a boy, but he had never dared go in the water. They took him down to the point in the river where it was deep enough to dive in and helped him into the water. At first, he refused to take his shoes off but they convinced him that it was dangerous to jump in fully clothed. Slowly he climbed down into the ice-cold river and was immediately comfortable with its cooling temperature and pleasant feel. For an hour he splashed around, smiling and making fun of himself before climbing out and driving back home in his tractor, barefoot. The following September he was dead.

When Marie had finished setting the table, she sat down under the shade of the largest tree to have a glass of water. She inspected her work and realised that the aesthetic of the table and the little yard had not changed since she was a girl and, later, when she married Jean-Michel and he had come to live and work with her on the farm, they had not changed a thing, only maintaining what was before and mending what may have been broken or damaged. The weeds still poked through the cobblestones which lay dusty upon the ground, the terracotta flowerpots still boasted bright geraniums and the vines of unknown grapes still climbed around the trellis which framed the yard. In the distance beyond the lane which led to their home, she could see the apple trees which they harvested each year to make their cider. The sweet, fresh juice would be pressed from them in the old wooden press and left to ferment over the winter months. With spring came a new season of cider and merriment and now that it was summer, the acidic, cold, flat cider was well appreciated to quench the thirst of hard workers and to cut through the fatty meat of their lambs and pigs at the dinner table.

Throughout the morning, Ana basted the lamb with xipister, a mix of brine, vinegar, herbs and garlic, every 20 minutes or so and turned the carcasses over.

The guests began to arrive and brought a bottle of wine from Paris and some anchovies and olives from Spain. Both Ana and her mother embraced and kissed each guest and showed them into the dark kitchen where she opened a bottle of cider and gave them all large, simple beakers made of thin glass to drink it from, pouring a little into each glass from a height. The anchovies and olives she placed upon the table so that they may enjoy them as an aperitif before lunch. They talked about the heat of the day and how this summer had been unusually hot, and the group complained that they were hungover as they had

been out the night before in the town until late. Her mother disapproved greatly of this, not because she disapproved of drinking, but because she thought it good manners to turn up to lunch in good condition and with a good appetite for both food and drink. She herself had been looking forward to the meal and had not taken breakfast that morning so to not spoil her appetite. Were they not to finish the lamb, she thought, her and her daughter would find it difficult to consume it in the coming days.

Ana had, by now, almost finished roasting the lamb and had put on an apron and gloves to help carve them, which she did with an axe and a large boning knife. Under her apron, she wore a summer dress of simple faded blue and espadrille sandals. With the help of her brother, who had come home especially for the lunch, she placed the cooked lambs onto a large wooden table where she began to butcher them using the axe. Once in smaller pieces, she worked from leg to shoulder, taking meat from the bone and slicing it before stacking it onto large metal serving plates. Her mother had dressed the salads with a simple cider vinegar, salt and olive oil dressing and was placing them on the table along with several bottles of cold cider. Once the platters of lamb arrived, the busy chat of the diners softened to a chorus of cutlery and plates and the clinking of glasses.

RECIPE

Spit-roast Lamb

A piece of suckling lamb, shoulder or leg or larger
500ml cider vinegar
250ml brine (salted water)
A sprig of rosemary
A sprig of thyme
A whole espelette pepper
A head of garlic
Xipister

Leave to marinate for at least two weeks.

Begin in an oven at 130°C and roast for one hour. Baste every 15 minutes with xipister. Turn up the heat to 200°C and roast for a further 20–30 minutes, basting regularly. Let rest for around 15–20 minutes before carving and serving on a warmed serving plate.

Serve with a green salad.

The End and the Beginning of Love

It was the end of love. I spent the autumn pining
for a German girl who had spent the summer
days making love to me in my studio flat on
the sixth floor of a shabby old building on the
rue Jouye-Rouve, but who had gone back to
Cologne in September and not written to me
since, except to say that she was quite happy to
be home again. I lay in bed most days, smoking
cigarettes and thinking about her, and the days
we spent together in my room when I would
wake up early and make her coffee and run off
to the boulangerie under my flat to buy her
croissants for breakfast. She would cook dinner
later in the evening and rarely did we think it
necessary to leave those four walls. Clumsily, she
spilled squid ink on my favourite shirts which
she insisted on wearing and I just laughed at the
time. I had nothing to offer her but my undying
affection and I gave her it all. She was much
more interesting than me. She talked about thing
that I did not understand and I listened to
every word. I have always been sort of a boring
character. I have little to share or talk about with

others, and when I do speak, I normally regret it. I therefore spent the day listening to her opinions and ideas and making love to her in between times. On some warm summer nights we would go out late and take long walks down to the river and through the empty streets. On others we would sulk and fight when she told me that she would go back to Germany at the end of summer. Her leaving scared me, it felt like I was awaiting the end of a terminal illness. I wanted to squeeze every drop of life out of my time before it ended. We talked for hours on a bench under the plane trees until I got something stuck in my throat and we had to go home for a drink of water.

She didn't share my sadness for the end, she was looking forward to leaving Paris and to seeing her friends and family again. I had no friends or family that I cared to see or hear of. My family I had little contact with other than pleasantries from time to time. My friends I had abandoned in that hot summer and so none of them maintained a relationship with me. Now, when I felt her immense absence, I wandered the streets alone, calling into bookshops to browse the titles that caught my eye, and buying one, perhaps, which I would be too distracted to read. I chanced upon pretty cafés and bars where I would amuse myself for a moment with a glass of beer, or cycle to the other side of the city and back in pursuit of something even mildly

interesting to catch my attention. I had no one
to talk to and was engulfed by self-pity. Once,
I saw an old friend of mine while out walking in
Ménilmontant and he looked shocked, almost
scared, to see me. My dishevelled appearance,
scruffy hair and unclean clothes certainly did
not help. He failed to ask me of my relationship,
but made excuses that he was off to see a friend
and shouldn't be late. Off he pushed his bicycle
away from me.

Later, when it got cold in the winter months,
I missed her warmth in my bed. I sat with a
woollen jumper on in bed and read the same
poems over and over again. At night I would
drink alone in a bar, a different one each night
so no one might recognise me, and walked
home drunk and slept well.

It was this way that I got into cooking. I could
barely afford my drinking habit and I desperately
needed a part-time job in the evenings. I took
a few shifts at one of the bars I used to frequent
and, on top of my pay, I could help myself to
drink during working hours. I began to work
there more often and before I realised it I had quit
my day job in the library and had started
working full time in this dirty little kitchen with
an English man. He taught me many of the
skills of that class of people who toil in kitchens.
I learned to clean fish, to butcher meat, to roast
and fry and bake. I learned to make all sorts of
doughs and pastries and creams. I even learned

to make the squid ink sauce I had eaten almost a year before. The work was hard and the nights late, but I was not lonely any more. I became acquainted with people who would listen to me when I had something to share, and who I enjoyed listening to late into the night, when they would drink and laugh and tell stories.

I was unhappy to hear the English cook would leave. He had taught me so much and I did not want to think what might happen after his time in my life ended. He was replaced by a French girl. She was kind and generous to me. On some nights we would talk after work as we walked home, enjoying the warm weather. On one of these nights she told me that she would like to make dinner for me. I felt exhilarated by the idea. When we parted, I ran up the rue de Belleville and got home and turned the music up so loud that my neighbour came down to complain. The next day I went to her flat to eat. She made a ratatouille. I felt. I felt the food, the conversation, the night air coming in the window and the taste of the wine on my lips and the feeling of it in my belly. I had not felt for a long time. I listened to her, and she listened to me. It was the beginning of love.

RECIPE

Cuttlefish in its Ink

This dish can be made with squid, but I find cuttlefish less sweet than squid, which I don't find particularly good when stewed. Cuttlefish also has a more agreeable texture when cooked in this manner.

First you will need a fresh, line-caught cuttlefish. If the cuttlefish is not line caught then it will likely not contain ink. If it is fresh and line caught then its skin will appear colourful and vibrant and should even change colour when touched. If this happens then it is of excellent quality. To clean and butcher a cuttlefish, use a sharp knife to open the body where the bone is. Open it up completely and remove the insides. You will see a black ink pouch. Carefully cut this away and place in a bowl or small pot or container for later. Next use your hands to tear away the skin or membrane from the cuttlefish and discard. Slice the flesh into long strips. Separate the head and tentacles and any other meaty bits from the insides and discard the insides. Slice the rest into pieces. In the meantime, sauté at least four onions in olive oil with around three cloves of garlic, some peperoncino or cayenne pepper and a little carrot, green pepper or celery if you like. These should be ready in an hour of slow cooking. Once ready, add a glass of white wine and reduce completely, then add peeled tomatoes, bay leaves and the ink and cook for a further 20 minutes.

While you cook the sauce, fry the cuttlefish separately in a heavy pan with plenty of olive oil. Set aside the cuttlefish, drained of its oil, and add to the sauce to finish cooking – around one hour or whenever the cuttlefish is tender. Adjust the sauce with vinegar if it is too sweet and extra water if it is too thick.

This is good on its own or served with basmati rice, a boiled potato or chickpeas. Beware that ink will stain everything, including nice tablecloths, shirts, pots and plates if left uncleaned.

Hunger, Part I

Feargal had spent the afternoon with his mother in the Botanic Gardens in Belfast, a dull and rainy afternoon but they never did mind that. They would spend most of the time in the hothouses looking at tropical plants where he would admire the Venus flytraps. The houses had a warm, humid smell which would always stick with him for the rest of his life. The colours of Belfast being dulled by the incessant greyness of the weather meant that the sky, the white paint on the greenhouses and the tarmac pavements looked even greyer than had they been in another city. And in contrast the red brick of the buildings added some colour to the city, particularly the ornate old red brick of Queen's University and the buildings around the park. It was nice to come out here to see a well-kept part of the city. Most parts were looking very run-down and worse for wear these days and there were no ornate red brick buildings being built, only concrete ones which looked even worse than the grey skies and paving stones with moss growing out of them

and puddles with the cigarette butts floating
in them.

Feargal held his mother's hand and walked
through the park towards the bus stop. She
seemed very grown up to him, but she was still
young. Feargal was ten years old, and he was very
close to his mother. His father had been in
prison for nine of his ten years of life. They would
visit him each week but every time Feargal cried
and said he never wanted to go back there. The
iron gates, barbed wire and guards who spoke
aggressively to his mother scared him. His father
was a man he had little affection for; he had
never spent more than 30 minutes with him and
the man didn't take to children naturally. His
environment before gaol had been mostly men
anyway, and now it was only men. Even meeting
Feargal's mother was strange for him.

A pigeon was eating someone's chips from
a paper sheet which had been discarded by the
bus stop, the bus pulled up and it flew away,
unable to finish its lunch. Feargal wished his
mother would buy him chips for lunch but
didn't ask because the answer was always no, they
didn't have money to go buying chips, they'd
eat at home.

In the evenings, when he took his bath, she
would calculate all she had to pay and what
getting to the end of the month would cost her
and then she would close her eyes and swallow,
feeling her stomach tightening with the

knowledge that getting to the end of the month would be almost impossible. Many times, neighbours had noticed and brought groceries to the house or left money on the kitchen table for the heating or the rent. People were good like that in Belfast, they looked after one another. Whenever possible they would get a little help from the prisoner's dependents fund, but money was always short for everyone in those days.

The bus moved through the city and Feargal stared out the window while his mother read her book. She was studying Irish and the only free time she had to read was when she was on the bus or in the back of a black taxi and sometimes, if she was not too tired, at night in bed.

They were on the way to his granny's house to get his tea, which was in the New Lodge area of the city. Once they got off the bus, they walked the rest of the journey up to the New Lodge Road and into Upper Meadow Street. Walking in the rain meant that by the time that they arrived they were cold and wet and Feargal's shoes let in water every time he walked through a puddle, which was often in Belfast, particularly from those paving stones which were loose and splashed up water as you walked over them.

He took off his socks when he got in and hung them over the radiator and examined his feet which had gone white and wrinkly with the damp. His mother spoke to his granny quietly in the kitchen as he turned on the cartoons.

This was a nicer house than his own. It was small and dark but always had the heating on from October through to March and the living room was comfortable and there was always good food cooking.

His granny came into the room and announced she would be making some soda farls and would he like one, to which he replied that he would, smiling to let her know that he was well and happy. The soda farls don't take a second to make and quickly the women set about putting them together, his mother passing the flour, baking soda and buttermilk, while his grandmother mixed them to the right consistency and shaped them. Onto a warm pan they were placed and left to rise slowly. Meanwhile they made a pot of tea and sliced some cheese and opened a pot of pickled beetroot from Missus McNalley's down the road. His granny then stood at the back door smoking while his mother set the table and told her that she had to stop smoking, it would kill her one day. She responded by saying that there were much easier ways to be killed in Belfast and that she'd lasted this long.

She already had a stew made and she lit the stove to heat it up while she stood finishing the cigarette at the back door. After some moments passed, Feargal could smell the stew overwhelm the cigarette smoke and he realised he was hungry. They didn't eat much at his mother's house and he had only had Weetabix for breakfast before heading out for the day. He liked Weetabix. At the bottom of his street there was graffiti that read BRITISH ARMY BEWARE, THE IRA HAVE HAD THEIR WEETABIX. It made him think of his da and whether or not they got Weetabix in gaol. The farls, freshly risen, had come off the pan and were sliced open and lathered with butter. His granny brought them to the table and they all sat down together to have cheese and pickled beetroot and soda farls and after, a bowl of stew. The tea was steaming hot and warmed him through, making him forget about the rain outside. His mother smiled at him, asking did he like his farl and to thank his granny.

His granny turned the radio on; the news was on, the situation in the prison was getting worse, no compromise was being made by the British Government. The men inside had decided on a hunger strike to reach their demands. His granny held his hand and told him to eat up, his mother went out the back door, lit a cigarette and burst into tears.

RECIPE

Belfast Stew

I am calling this Belfast stew because it differs slightly to the Irish stew most people know as it is made with minced beef. I have only ever seen this in Belfast.

Onions
Carrots
Lard or vegetable oil
Minced beef
Floury potatoes
Beef stock or water

Chop the onions and cut the carrots into rounds. Gently fry the onions and carrots in lard or vegetable oil.

Take a pound or two of minced beef and add it to the onions. Cook on a higher heat, stirring until browned, and then add some peeled potatoes, chopped in halves or quarters. Add stock or water to cover. Cook until the potatoes are very tender.

Better served the following day.

Soda Farls

Soda farls are only eaten in Ulster and are mostly confined to what is now called the North of Ireland. In the South of Ireland, 'soda bread' refers to what we would call wheaten bread, a loaf of mixed grain to be baked and sliced, which is particularly good with soft salty butter or jam. Soda farls are often filled with bacon, eggs and sausage to make a considerable breakfast. But they can also be served simply buttered, with jam, or with melted cheese.

Put around 300g of flour in a bowl and add a teaspoon of bicarbonate of soda and a pinch of salt. Add enough buttermilk to bring it all together and form into a ball. Flatten the ball so that you have a round disk about two centimetres deep.

Cook on a dry pan until well cooked on both sides. It should take around 20 minutes. You can finish it in the oven if you are worried about it burning before the cooking is finished. Eat immediately. These do not keep terribly well.

Daydreams

Paco stood at the bow of the small fishing boat as it approached the pier of the village of Ziburu. It was early morning and still dark, but they had already filled their nets and were returning to land without hesitation. The sea had been rough, and besides they had no room left in their nets for more fish, although they could have had many more tonnes had they a bigger boat. They were fishing bonito in small nets, which was the old way of fishing in that area since anyone could remember. Paco had arrived twenty-five years previously, a refugee from Francoist Spain. He lived among other refugees, in precarious jobs, socialising in the back of dark, quiet port bars and living in a modest apartment in an old building which was in great need of renovation. He threw the mooring line over the bollard on the quay and let down the buoys to pull the boat closer in. The fish was taken laboriously from the nets and placed in boxes which were pulled up onto the pier. Just the effort of lifting and carrying these boxes was enough for a day's work. As the men worked, the sun rose and illuminated

the harbour. Larrune, the hill that overlooked
the village and surrounding areas, was still
dark and an orange sun glowed behind it. From
the mountain, down the Urdazuri river and all
through the valley and the flat plain at Senpere,
the land was being taken out of the darkness of
the night and into the gentle early morning light.

His wife, Anamari, was preparing breakfast
for him when he arrived home and took off his
working clothes and boots. He changed into a
shirt and trousers and sat down at the kitchen
table. She greeted him with a kiss on the cheek
and put coffee in front of him and a plate of
fried eggs and boudin noir. He poured a glass
of red wine to drink with the meal then, having
finished, a coffee from a percolator on the
table. After, to 'rinse the glass', as he put it, a
little Cognac. Anamari watched him eat and
drank her morning coffee. She did not eat
in the mornings and was about to go out to
the market, where she thought she might have
a croissant in the little bar that served the
vendors and shoppers. After eating, he went
to bed straight away and fell into a deep sleep
which he would not awake from until well
after midday.

Anamari saw that he had left a plastic bag of
fish in the fridge. He often brought home fish he
had taken from the boat, a catch that was too
small or bits and pieces they didn't sell. It wasn't
unknown for other fishermen from other boats

and port workers to give him something to take home either. Later she would make a soup with them when she returned from the market.

When he woke, Paco made his way lazily into the kitchen and made some more coffee. He then washed and shaved his tired face. He sported a large, bushy moustache and was almost totally bald except for some short hair at the sides. He left the apartment where Anamari was preparing dinner for that evening and walked the short distance to the bar in the village square where he found his friends playing cards in the back. Although the day, by now, was bright and sunny, the interior of the bar was dark and cool. No music played in the bar, there was just the sound of men's voices and the placing of cards and glasses on a table. Some men wore black berets and some peered through spectacles at their hands; others were heard to cough as they smoked their cigarettes, whose smoke inevitably escaped up the large chimney to the side of the room.

In the back was a little kitchen where fishermen prepared food for each other. There were three men inside debating over which way to cook a ttoro. On wooden boards they held fish and sliced off heads and fillets with sharp butcher's knives, frying onions all the while.

Smoke filled the room until it was difficult to see properly, and the sun outside stood waiting at the door, afraid to come in. Paco and his comrades spoke in low voices about the fish

caught last night, about the expected catch today
and what the weather had been like. But this was
only small talk that the men used to avoid their
real preoccupations. Many were on the run
and the bullet holes in the bar's wall were proof
of the fact that they were still not safe and that
some knew where they were. These were men,
many of whom had been savagely tortured,
whose worries went beyond what many others
considered life's trials. Paco himself still bore
marks upon his back from when he was taken
for ten days and interrogated by the Guardia
Civil. He was permanently half deaf since they
hit him so hard on the head during that time
that he lost his hearing. In those days he had
lost sense of time, being kept awake night and
day in a windowless cell. He had no idea where
he was. He only looked for ways to take his
own life, death being the only salvation from
his barbarous torturers. When he was released,
he left for the French side of the border and
never looked back. He was still afraid of the
kidnappings he had heard about, and the
paramilitary mercenaries, paid to assassinate
men like him. But at least he was not under
immediate risk and could disappear into these
little port bars and let the wine numb his
memories of what had happened to him.

The men had now finished preparing the ttoro.
Paco snapped out of his daydreaming and was
told to clear the cards from the table as the pot

was about to arrive. Shallow dishes were shared out and the ladle helped to splash a portion on each plate. They ate as hungry men eat who have been enduring the smells of a well-cooked meal all afternoon. It quickly disappeared from their dishes only to be replaced by more. In a few hours many of them would be going back to sea. Come nightfall, they must be sailing under the stars and searching for the bonito they couldn't catch the night before. Only then did Paco feel really at ease, safe and apart from a world that had been so hard.

RECIPE

Ttoro Fish Stew

This is a fish stew which comes from the Basque province of Lapurdi and in particular from the mainly working-class fishing village of Ziburu (or Ciboure in French) where most of the fishermen live and work. Originally, it was a stew made with the heads of fish given to the fishermen's wives. More recently it has been turned into an expensive restaurant dish which includes langoustines and clams. This is my own recipe, based on my time living there and what locals may consider a traditional dish, if not the original, which may have been closer to a soup.

Monkfish
Hake
Conger eel
Gurnard
Small rock fish
Parsley
Bay leaves or leek trimmings
Onions
Garlic
Olive oil
Carrot

Pimiento chorizero, dried pepper or conserved tomato
Piment d'Espelette, smoked paprika or saffron
Wine
Floury potatoes

Take a selection of these fish, fillet them and
make a fish broth with the bones and heads. For
the broth, simply place the well-cleaned fish,
free of any blood or guts, into a large pot with
cold water, and if available some parsley stalks,
bay leaves or leek trimmings. Bring the pot to
a simmer and skim off the froth created with a
ladle or large spoon. Simmer for 30 minutes and
allow to cool.

Meanwhile make the base of the stew. Sauté
onions and garlic slowly in olive oil, adding a
little carrot if you like. It should cook slowly
until the onions are tender, for a minimum of
30 minutes, but better still for an hour. Next
add a little conserved tomato or, more properly,
some pimiento chorizero or dried pepper. You
can also add some piment d'Espelette, smoked
paprika or saffron. Add some dry white wine
and reduce. Peel some floury potatoes and then
'break' them using a small paring knife, causing

them to break into irregular pieces. Add the potatoes and enough of the stock to cover.

Once the potatoes are cooked, add the fish fillets, chopped into pieces, and poach until just cooked. Take note that the temperature of the liquid may go down, depending on how much fish you add, and may need a while to come back up to a simmer. The consistency should be one of intact pieces of fish and potato floating in a broth, not a purée!

Serve with freshly minced parsley.

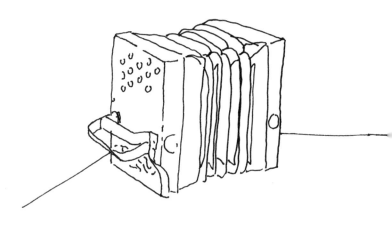

A Scent on the Air

In a small cottage in northeast Donegal lived Lucy
Campbell. She was in her last years, or so she
told everyone, and she did little else but potter
around the house and yard, never leaving her
domain. The house was a bungalow which had
a front door leading straight into the living room.
It was quite long and encompassed bedrooms
on both sides of the living room and an indoor
toilet, a barn and a turf shed. The roof was made
of thatch and inside the living room was dark
and smoky, by cause of the small windows which
were rarely left open, apart from on particularly
warm summer days. She looked after chickens
and a goat. Her days were spent growing roses,
which framed the arch above the gate leading to
the house and which grew along trellises pinned
onto the building, and, when possible, or in the
mood, making cheese with the goat's milk. She
was known in the area for selling eggs and goat's
cheese and people would send their children to
the house to buy from her. She also sold poitín,
which was made by men in the hills behind the
house, good places to hide from the customs

men or the guards. There were stories of men coming to the house late at night to sell her the spirits and being invited in, not to emerge again until morning time, when, in the dull half light, they would be spotted by a neighbour sauntering down the road away from her house. Children were never sent to buy poitín, of course, but their parents were aware of where they needed to ask had they need for some at home.

The next cottage on looked much the same as Lucy's and there lived Eimer with her young son Cathal. Eimer was much younger than Lucy and had moved into the cottage only a year previous. She had come from Derry and been offered the house to live in with her young son as she might have some peace and quiet to write. She had gotten to know Lucy by calling into the house from time to time and chatting with her in the garden on the good days during May and June. One such day, she had arrived to find Lucy totally naked, sunbathing on a patch of grass beside the chicken coup. Eimer had let out a shriek and startled Lucy, who looked up out of her sunglasses to see who was breaking the peace. She said simply, 'Oh, it's only you Eimer!' and went back to her original position. Eimer had come looking for a bottle of poitín to bring as a present back to Derry and Lucy reluctantly got up and dressed herself in a loose frock and went to find the bottle. She wandered into the turf shed and rummaged around among the thatch and beams for a while, finally pulling out a bottle of clear, unmarked liquid. She uncorked it, smelled it and winked at Eimer in approval.

Lucy played the concertina and there were many nights, when Eimer had first arrived, when she could hear music and laughter coming from Lucy's house and saw lights on inside until late into the next morning. One day Eimer asked if Lucy had had a party the night before and Lucy replied that she didn't know what she was on about, but if she wanted to hear a bit of the old music, she was welcome whenever she heard it.

Eimer had little opportunity to leave the house in the direction of the music as she looked after her son alone, but this weekend he was to stay with her family in Derry as it was his cousin's birthday and he had pleaded to stay. At ten years old, her son Cathal was already anxious for independence. Ever since he was old enough to walk around alone, he loved to go over to Lucy's house with a few punts in his hand and buy some eggs, which he would put into some baskets and balance on his shoulders on a long stick. It was a contraption he had made to transport the eggs. Being an only child and living in such a remote place, he spent his days inventing things and playing alone in the garden and hills behind the house, chasing wild goats around and pretending he was a character out of the stories his mother would tell him when he lay in bed at night. Cú Chulainn, Fionn and Na Fianna,

Diarmuid and Grainne and Queen Maebh. But
now he was becoming frustrated with such a
solitary life and wanted, more and more, to stay
in Derry and meet his cousins and their friends.

Before driving her son to Derry, Eimer had
asked him to go and fetch some eggs and to ask
Lucy if she would mind if they paid next week
for them. She hadn't been paid what she had
agreed with the local newspaper yet and she was
now struggling to get to the end of the month.
She drove the hour's drive home as the sun was
setting on the Urris Hills and the little car wound
its way through the old bog roads which took
her over Mamore Gap and round hairpin bends
into the valley below, an orange light making the
patchwork countryside take on the colour of
the copper tips which grew wild across the hillside
and on the sides of the lanes along with fuchsia,
foxglove and fern.

Once she arrived at the lonely little cottage,
she came in through the door and set about
lighting a fire. She was hungry now and saw the
eggs in the basket upon the table. Methodically,
she lit the stove and set a heavy pan to heat,
breaking the eggs into a bowl and gently beating
them with a fork. Dropping them into the
foaming butter and pushing them around a little
with a wooden spoon, she reached into the
cupboard and found a bottle of wine. Once
ready, she folded the omelette onto a plate and
sat alone at the kitchen table with the omelette

and a glass of wine. As she sat at the table eating
her omelette in silence, she heard the sweet
concertina music she sometimes heard coming
from Lucy Campbell's house. Peering through
the little window, she saw lights on in the house
and smoke drifting from the chimney. There
were noises of men talking and the odd shout
which interrupted the music.

Quickly, she put her coat on and made for the
door, dressing in her boots and a large woollen
jumper she used for working in the garden.
She made her way down the lane and into Lucy's
garden, passed the rose bushes, and gently
pushed the open door. Inside were mostly men,
standing around drinking from china cups, some
with bottles of black stout.

'Come in,' Lucy said, 'and close that door for
you'll let the heat out.' Lucy was sitting on a
chair by the large hearth with the concertina
on her lap. Some of the men joined her seated
and others, standing, were out of breath and had
clearly been dancing.

'Will you have a drink?' asked Lucy.

'Eh, yes please. Have you a glass of wine?' Eimer
felt ridiculous as soon as she asked it. Lucy simply
looked at her bemused and laughed. She handed
her a china cup and poured a little clear liquid
into it. It burned her insides but was somehow
sweet. The music started up again, men battered
their feet on the ground, one hummed along
to the tune, another played the spoons to the

rhythm. Again and again they danced and sang and drank and told stories and then drank again. Eimer did not remember what time she left the house but the cold night air gave her a rush to the head and then began to sober her up again. Carefully and slowly she walked home, tripping from time to time on the grass which grew along the middle of the road.

When she woke, early in the morning, she looked out upon the garden, still with beads of dew on every plant, and across the little lane she could see a man walking home, whistling, trying to put his coat on.

A Scent on the Air

RECIPE

An Omelette For One

Probably the most important factor in making an omelette is a good omelette pan. I highly recommend buying a good-quality carbon steel pan. This must be seasoned by heating it and applying oil several times before it forms a natural seal which will prevent the omelette from sticking. They should never be washed with water and cleaned simply by wiping with a rag or paper. Keep one pan for making omelettes.

For one person, beat three eggs in a bowl gently and heat your pan. Once the pan is hot, add a good dollop of butter and let it melt, moving the pan a little to help it. Season the eggs with sea salt and, if you like, a dash of vinegar, and add them to the hot pan. Immediately turn down the heat and vigorously move the pan in circles over the heat. You will see the omelette forming. Use a wooden spatula to move the edges inward and tip the pan from side to side. Once the eggs are almost cooked, roll the omelette away from you to the other side of the pan. It should have no browning. Tip it off the pan and onto a plate and eat immediately.

A glass of wine is recommended.

A Gardener

On the hill upon which the neighbourhood of
Belleville and its surrounding area stood was a
small community allotment in which Monsieur
Fourcade had his little patch of land. Among the
roses and hydrangeas he loved to grow, he had
a little patch of vegetables and herbs which he
grew to feed himself. Monsieur Fourcade rarely
bought vegetables and almost never bought
meat. He had worked as a bus driver his whole
life and had retired on a modest pension which
meant that after paying rent he had almost
nothing left to live on. He therefore bought
rice and beans and chickpeas and flour at the
local Indian and North African grocers and
complemented it with vegetables from his little
garden. The only luxuries that he permitted
himself were to drink a coffee from time to time
in the bar near his house and to buy wine once
a month, when he received his pension, so he
could have a glass at the end of the day.

It was on one of these days, having coffee
in his local bar, that he had met Claire. He
had been sitting alone, as usual, reading his

newspaper and stirring sugar into his coffee when she asked him where he had bought his coat. He could not have said that he didn't find her immediately attractive. She was much younger than he was, perhaps still in her twenties, and well dressed. Her dark hair was tied in a bun and a fringe covered her forehead. She wore red lipstick and a red jumper and blue jeans.

He looked at the coat and back at her, stuttering, unable to understand why she had any interest at all in it. He couldn't, in fact, say where he had got the coat. He had perhaps found it or bought it a long time ago in a second-hand shop. It was a big clumsy coat he wore for gardening and was useful because it was resistant to the rain and had many large pockets for putting tools and seeds and what-not in.

He peered at her through his glasses. His beard unshaven for three days, his face beginning to look wrinkled and tired and his hair, once black, different shades of grey and white now. Not knowing what to do he asked why. She responded that she thought it looked very good and would like to find one just like it. After a few seconds of hesitation, he took the coat off and offered it to her. She refused and said she could never take the coat. He thought that perhaps the coat smelled or was too shabby or, he, too dirty-looking for her, to even consider wearing it after him and was ashamed of his offer.

'Do you drink wine?' she asked.

'I do,' he replied timidly.

'I run a wine shop. I'll trade you wine for the coat,' she said.

And so it was settled. That's how Monsieur Fourcade and Claire began their relationship. She told him to give her the coat and that she would provide him with wine whenever he needed to fill up his bottle. Each week, he would visit her, and she would fill the bottle from a barrel she kept in the shop. They would talk about plants and books and music and films and then he would leave as soon as another customer came in who she had to attend to.

On many occasions, he would bring her flowers from the garden, commenting that he had to trim them and didn't know of anyone who he could offer them to and since she had a shop maybe she would appreciate them for the counter. He did not know it, but her favourite part of the week was to receive his visits and his flowers. One day he asked her if she would like to visit his garden, which she enthusiastically accepted.

The allotments were surrounded by walls and gates and he needed a key to let himself in. People grew many things, from courgettes to raspberry bushes to cutting flowers. They walked to the far end of the garden where he had his little plot. It was neat and tidy and well cared for. Pretty flowers shared beds with ripe tomatoes, beans and spinach. She bent down and examined them closely. The soil was rich and dark, she remarked. The fact that she worked in wine meant that she knew the value of good soil and that only good farming methods brought about good, healthy soil. Insects could be seen crawling and flying around and as she admired the bed, Monsieur Fourcade picked slugs off his cabbages and threw them into the compost heap.

The day was mild, neither sunny nor cold and wet. He did not say much but let her look for herself. Instead, he sat and smoked a rolled cigarette on an upturned plastic crate and looked at the sky. After a minute of daydreaming, he was startled out of it by her voice saying that she must go and let him get on with his work.

'I have no work,' he said. 'I'm retired now.'

'What do you call all this?' she asked.

'Therapy?' he replied. She smiled.

'Would you like to have lunch with me?' he asked her in a moment of bravery and madness.

'Today?' she asked.

'Sorry, I'm sure you already have plans, it's your day off, you must be with friends or such.'

'No, I'm free to have lunch today,' she replied.

He didn't know why he had asked her to have lunch, he had no pride in his cooking skills and found it embarrassing to cook for others. It was, simply, that he didn't want her to leave. It also began to dawn on him that he had no food in the house other than some rice he had bought in La Chapelle the week before and the odd conserve from the garden and some dried herbs, onions and garlic. And so, realising that he had no money left to buy anything, he began to look around his little garden for something he could cook.

He plucked a few runner beans off the vine and put them in a little wicker basket he kept around. A few tomatoes too, and walked in the direction of his home. Claire caught up with him and followed behind; she insisted that she stop at the shop to take a bottle of wine.

His flat was very sparse and simple. He was not a man who had money for, or interest in, material things. He had no television, no computer and no sofa. A simple rectangular wooden table sat in the middle of the main room and to the side was an old kitchen. Even the kitchen utensils were sparse. He washed some rice in a basin and left it to soak. As he did this, he chopped tomatoes, sliced onions and minced garlic. Then he put a pot on the boil and began to sauté the onions in a heavy casserole. Monsieur Fourcade was not used to drinking at lunch. It made him tired and anyway he could never permit himself to do so as the cost of wine was so much. She had brought a special bottle she had explained, something which a friend of hers had made. A simple wine, young and light, but special to her as her friend had made it and there were not many of them. She poured it out into the little water glasses he had and passed him one to sip while he cooked and they chatted.

He added the tomatoes to the onions and continued to cook them a little and blanched the runner beans in the boiling water. Claire watched how he effortlessly cooked this simple meal of garden bounty, cleaning as he went, organising, tidying, sipping his wine from time to time. He rarely spoke, letting her do much of the talking.

Finally, he poured the rice into the onions and tomatoes and covered it with a little water and a lid and let it simmer. The runner beans were removed from the water and cooked with some garlic and chilli which he had managed to grow the year before and dried. Once the rice was ready, he let it rest and set the table.

The table had a plastic cover with flowers on it. He laid out some knives and forks and plates and a serving spoon. He had forgotten to buy bread, no matter, they had rice after all. The simple water glasses held the wine and, as they sat down to eat the pilaf rice and stewed runner beans, they clinked the glasses in ceremonious but silent appreciation of their friendship.

RECIPE

Riz Pilaf

Basmati rice
Onions
Olive oil
Tomatoes
Butter

Set the rice to soak for 30 minutes in cold water, changing the water several times until clear.

Meanwhile, in a heavy pot, sauté the onions for 30 minutes and add the tomatoes towards the end.

Add the rice, enough water or chicken stock to cover it by around a centimetre, place the lid on, and cook on a low heat or in the oven for 20 minutes or until the rice is cooked, adding more liquid if necessary.

Once cooked, place some little cubes of butter on top of the rice. Let it rest for 15 minutes before eating, forking through the rice before serving. Serve with more olive oil at the table.

This alone is a divine lunch on a summer's day with a glass of wine outside, in the shade of a tree, or in a cold kitchen with the door left open.

Runner Beans in Garlic and Chilli

Runner beans
Garlic
Peperoncino
Olive oil

Boil the runner beans in salted water for around 10-15 minutes. Drain off the water and leave to cool and release any liquid.

Meanwhile, cook some garlic and dried peperoncino or any dried chilli in plenty of good olive oil until the garlic is just starting to brown. Add the beans and cook for a further 10-15 minutes on a low heat, stirring from time to time.

Serve as a dish in itself with good bread to mop up.

An Urge

The parlour room had been full all day with some
kind of party Katie's father had been throwing
for his friends in the business community, or the
hunting club, or the philanthropic society he
chaired, she wasn't sure. Anyway they were all
the same men. The smell of tobacco smoke and
whiskey still lingered in the room by the time
Katie walked in to find the men had all left for
supper in the golf club, including Mr Jackson,
Sam to her, who she had wanted to chat
with but would never dare to in front of her
father. She and Sam had been seeing each other
for six months now. On any given evening he
might send for her, or seeing her in the town
earlier that morning, arrange to meet her out
by the bridge, where he'd pick her up in his
new car and they would go for a drive together
out towards Wicklow. He said he liked to show
her the countryside but they rarely left the car.
As soon as he'd parked in some empty car park
or on a lonely byway he would reach over and
kiss her and not a minute would pass before he
began lifting up her skirt and, as he grew hot and

frustrated, pulled his tie down and took off
his jacket and climbed over the gearstick to
get at her. Generally she found this all quite
unimpressive, but she knew he liked it and so
she let him have his way with her for the
next ten minutes until it was all over. At thirty
years old, he was ten years her senior. They
had decided to keep the affair a secret at
Sam's suggestion, as he insinuated that her
father would not understand or condone their
relationship on account of their difference
in age.

His father was also a local businessman and
was liked by everyone Katie knew. He was the
owner of the town's hotel and bar and ran
several other affairs apart from that, which Katie
was not interested in hearing about. Sam didn't
like to talk about his father and instead simply
chit-chatted about town gossip and sports
with Katie until they arrived wherever Sam had
decided to drive them. On the way back he would
talk much less but would kiss her and smile at her
with his big, charming smile and red, flustered
cheeks from time to time while he negotiated
the bends along the old country roads.

Back in the parlour room, Katie sat alone and
disappointed he hadn't come to say hello. She
didn't see why he couldn't be seen doing that
at the very least. But she was sure he would say
that it would look too strange for him to go
looking for her and that it would have been

uncouth of her to enter into the room with all
the men while father was hosting a party. She
closed her eyes and thought of his lovely smile.
Oh what a lovely, handsome man he was, she
thought, he really must love her.

Her mother was in the kitchen clearing things
away, when Katie heard her voice calling her
name from the other side of the house. She
looked out of the tall, shuttered window onto the
lawn and the rich barley fields beyond, almost
ready to harvest, observing how the morning's
rains still sat upon the geranium leaves in the
terracotta pots and listened to the birdsong of
early evening as they went looking for worms
and grubs in the grass below the apple tree.
Her mother's voice again. She ran off into the
kitchen to find a piece of cake waiting for her.
Her mother always said it was the mark of a
civilized household to take high tea like the
English did. And so she would sit with her
daughter in the early evening to partake in a
little cake or sandwiches or perhaps an egg or
piece of fish and a pot of tea between them.

She sniffed at the cake. Orange, she thought.
She did love an orange cake, almost as much
as she loved Sam, she pondered. Katie gobbled
down the morsel of cake to her mother's
outrage, as a young lady should never gobble
anything. Although her mother had always
corrected her on such important matters, such
as what speed a lady should eat at, her daughter

had never understood this simple instruction and had continued to eat food like some ravenous peasant who had been out labouring in the fields. She worried that poor Katie would always fall to these simple pleasures and act in such an animalistic way. Katie's mother was well aware of her gallivanting with Mr Jackson. She viewed it with the same disdain she viewed her daughter eating cake. Would she ever learn to be patient, she thought.

The tea slurped down and the cake gobbled, Katie left the kitchen satisfied. More satisfied, in fact, than when she had finished gallivanting with Mr Jackson. There was something she enjoyed about doing the gobbling and not being gobbled, as she saw it. She left the house by the back door and went to sit on the swing by the oak tree, near the back of the garden. She wondered if she would be called upon tonight by her love, and if later she would have leftovers of cold chicken in aspic for her supper, which she would devour.

RECIPE

Chicken in Aspic

The day after making a poached chicken, you may reduce some of the cooking liquid and add gelatine sheets or a veal trotter, if you have one.

Cut the chicken into pieces and add it to a terrine dish or pan loaf tin. Pour over the gelatinous stock and refrigerate for at least twelve hours.

Turn out and slice to serve cold. Perhaps with a potato salad or some toast.

Whitby Orange Cake

I call this Whitby orange cake because my mother does, and I quite like to continue the tradition. It has nothing particular about it from Whitby, other than she got the recipe off a man who was working in a café in Whitby.

Boil two large oranges for two hours, changing the water half way through, then cool and put through a food mill.

Beat five eggs with 250g of sugar until pale. Then add 250g of ground almonds, one teaspoon of baking powder and the orange pulp.

Bake for one hour at 180°C or 160°C in a fan oven.

Hunger, Part II

Just past the town, on the left-hand side, not far from the old church, was a place they called the Famine Village. It was abandoned and overgrown and now resembled a small wood, maybe left over from long ago when the country was covered in such trees. It was not, however. It was only a few generations ago that people lived and farmed that little townland. Christy had potato drills in the fields below and would dig and plant in its shadow. He had been told stories by the old people, some of whom could remember what had happened, of when the roadsides were littered with bodies of people who had perished on their way to the emigration boat or who had been walking to the Big House in search of food. Green leaked from their mouths as they lay dying; they had been eating grass, like animals in the field, to stay alive. Their animals, of course, were long dead, as were their weakest children, and when they got to the Big House they were turned away for fear of fever and contamination.

He sometimes imagined those ghostly shapes moving through the countryside, lying down

to die in the fields like his dog when it hid itself
behind the turf shed before dying, as he dug
the disturbed beds and harvested what he had
planted earlier in the year to take home. He had
seen emaciated shapes in the parish before.
He could imagine their faces, the same faces
some of the old people had who had subsisted
on very little most of their lives, one bad harvest
or rent hike away from destitution. They had
escaped famine by a generation but had never
ceased to be peasants on poor land.

Now Christy farmed that same boggy land
and managed to harvest potatoes twice a year
from it. In May the land was still sodden from
the rain. It had begun to shine and the weather
had been gentle on him for the past three
weeks, but this did not mean that the ground
was not still sodden against his tattered boots
and that he did not come home each evening
and put his shoes against the slowly dying fire
in hope that they would be dry by morning.
Those embers could never dry the insides of
leather boots, tormented by tears and holes
and pulled stitching. At night his children ran
barefoot around the cottage whilst he sat by
the fire with men and women who spoke of
revenge for those times. They met often in his
house and came in the dead of night over the
back road from the hill to rap lightly upon the
back door and enter into the badly lit room.
They conspired over pipe smoke and tea to plot

and scheme until they had the British out and the land back in their hands. They were hungry men; one by one many dropped off via the boat to England or America. The oldest of them had seen their rebellion put down, but they told the younger men across the fireside to keep faith, that the Organisation would triumph over England in the end, it was only a matter of time and circumstances. The Land War had happened and it was a sign that the people were ready to fight and as they sat talking and storytelling in Gaeilge late into the night, the young men listened with intense interest.

They were offered soup and bread as they talked and both men and women sat around singing and storytelling. Few barriers were available in those cramped houses; had the children been old enough to care, they might have listened to the plotting as well, and so all sexes and ages joined in on the treason. The soup warmed their bellies after the long walk over the hills and so loosened the conversation and by the time the men left, they felt full and happy and believed that perhaps they would win one day.

The next day Christy put his sodden boots on again and walked the lonely road to his potato drill. No men working to salute him on his way, all had left but one neighbour. He dug alone on the wet mountain slope, a wind blowing in from the bay which threatened rain. Winning felt much further away than last night. His belly

was empty again by midday. To reinvigorate
his courage, he felt into his pocket for a boiled
potato and began to peel it, then bit off half and
swallowed, washing it down with some milk.
He thought of the warm soup the night before
and tried to forget the thought, his labour
beating his sore body into submission, his mind
blank of thoughts; of soup or rebellion.

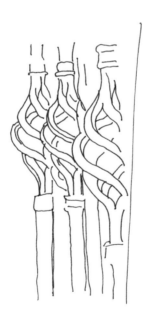

RECIPE

Irish Country Soup

An Irish country soup has no exact recipe but it's something I have found boiling away in many country homes while passing by on my travels through the country. It usually has lots of white or black pepper and a distinct taste of celery and plenty of barley.

I would use: celery, carrots, potatoes, leeks, onions, parsley, red lentils, split peas and barley and a beef bone with a bit of meat on it. Remember to soak the dried ingredients the night before and then just simmer everything together.

Fireworks

A cold wind blew through the open window as Malen stood smoking and watching the crowds gather in the streets below. Patxi asked her to finish and close it or they'd freeze. She stepped outside onto the balcony and closed the door behind her. The room in which they lived was practical and had none of the luxuries of many homes in the city. It was furnished simply with a table and two chairs; many books were arranged on shelves on the walls, piles on the floor and again upon a desk on the other side of the room. Near the desk lay two armchairs and upon it sat a digital radio. The kitchen had no cupboards or drawers and was open to the living room. Plates were stacked in a wooden rack above the sink and on shelves sat many pots and pans made of stainless steel, copper, terracotta, cast iron and iron. From the shelves hung hooks with vegetable mills, strainers, colanders, dried peppers, garlic, bushels of bay and chilli tied together by string. Patxi was there preparing the salt cod for the dinner. He was a large and quite unattractive man, but his nice manner gave him

a charm which made up for that. His girlfriend
Malen was as far from beauty as she was ugliness
and they spent their days reading, cooking
and talking without a care given to beauty and
vanity. He was dressed in a large, checkered shirt
which hung over his belly and oversized cotton
trousers which did not look uncomfortable and
therefore suited him as best as possible. He
wore no shoes but walked around in his socks,
cooking and listening to the radio. They were
both the same age at thirty-two and had known
each other since primary school. They had
grown up together and their union had been
quite natural to them both. On most evenings,
they would take a walk together around the
old town and perhaps pop in for a little drink
on their way home to one of their friends' bars.
Then they would go home so Patxi could prepare
dinner as he liked to do at the end of the day,
while Malen would read her books and smoke
cigarettes by the window. Today had not been
much different from other days. They had gone to
the market and bought some vegetables for the
soup and then for a drink with some friends
before heading home to make dinner. Normally
on occasions such as these, friends and family
would gather to eat together before heading out
for the night's festivities. Malen and Patxi,
however, felt no need for the company of others
and instead preferred to have a quiet, simple
meal, share a bottle of wine and go to bed early.

For this night he had been de-salting the bacalao for three days, changing the water in which it was soaking twice per day. He was making a pil-pil sauce which was a speciality of his, since it was technically difficult to achieve and he had mastered the technique. First, he made the soup, which was to be leek and potato. It was a simple soup, and it did not merit too much complication. Only good vegetables and olive oil. The potatoes were peeled and then cracked apart with a little paring knife like his mother had shown him to do. The leeks were washed inside and out and chopped up. He boiled them in enough water to cover and added some good olive oil and sea salt. It would take 30 minutes.

Patxi left the little kitchenette and kissed his partner on the head. He took his keys from the dresser and left to go to his little storage unit below. This was usually for keeping prams and bicycles but instead he kept bottles of wine and cider and some conserves. He took a jar of preserved tuna and a bottle of white wine from the shelf, locked the door behind him and walked up the stairs again. Eagerly, he opened the bottle and tasted the slightly cloudy contents. It was a wine made by an uncle of his in the hills near Guernica and it smelled of reduction, which he liked in the whites. His uncle had never read anything about what wine should be or shouldn't be or how it should be made, but he was shown how to do so by his grandfather and continued to make a small number of bottles each year from their little vineyard on a steep slope not far from the sea. He poured a glass and gave it to Malen who was by now inside and sitting on an armchair listening to the radio in French. She liked to listen to the radio in French and found the Spanish radio lacking in sophistication and the Basque radio far too provincial for her liking.

She smelled the wine and commented that it wasn't bad for a simple farmer, smiling to herself.

Patxi went about making a *pintxo* of tuna and thinly sliced onion on a piece of bread and brought her one, eating his standing at the counter, chin running with oil and hands too. He was forced to run the tap and wash before facing Malen again. They chatted and drank the wine while the soup boiled. Then he returned to the kitchen. He patted dry the thick slices of cod and began to fry sliced garlic and some whole cayenne peppers in olive oil. Once the garlic was browned, he removed it all with a slotted spoon and allowed the oil to cool. He placed the cod into the oil and reheated it gently. As the cod cooked in the shallow pool, it began to release a white liquid, which he watched for. Once this began to seep out of the cooking fish he took the pan – stainless steel, round and shallow – by both its handles and rhythmically moved it in circular motions, emulsifying the white into the oil. The end result appeared to

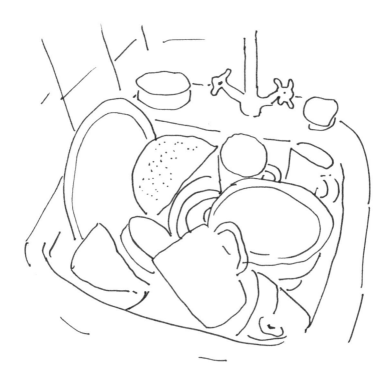

have a loose mayonnaise texture. Promptly, he added a little finely chopped parsley along with the garlic and cayenne previously removed. When the fish was cooked he left it aside to be gently reheated when needed and served the soup on their small, fold-out Formica table, serving it with a ladle from the pot, Malen first, into her shallow bowl.

After dinner, they heard fireworks explode in the sky outside and the bands began to play. They opened the window and walked out onto the balcony, wrapped in heavy jumpers and blankets, each holding a glass of Irish whiskey which they both loved.

All over the city people were singing, playing, drinking and revelling. It rang out like a great vibration through the whole town. The sound of the drinkers in the streets below was joyful and busy. They sipped their whiskey and saluted the evening before turning in for the night.

As they undressed, they sat at either side of the bed in silent exhaustion after the meal. Neither had the energy or desire to suggest making love; they had long stopped making love in spite of themselves on quiet nights like these. Forgetting to close the window shutters, their pale bodies, plump and round, covered with shirts and warm socks, shivered before falling asleep, in a room lit by moonlight and fireworks.

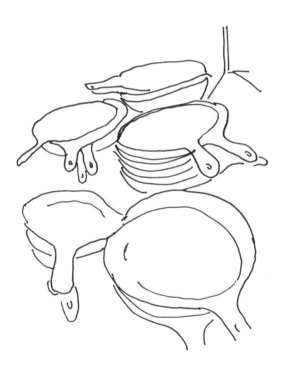

RECIPE

Tuna Conserve

A whole bonito tuna
Sea salt
Plenty of good-quality olive oil
Jars for preserving with new lids (jam jars are ideal)
A large pot which will fit the jars in

Ask your fishmonger to butcher the fish into fillets and belly, removing the skin, bones and bloody-red parts between the fillets.

Salt moderately with sea salt and leave for an hour or so in the fridge. Next rinse thoroughly the fillets and pat them dry with a tea towel. Sterilize the jars by boiling them for a moment and leaving them to drain. Once cool enough to handle, dry thoroughly with a clean towel. Alternatively you can use a good, hot dishwasher or a sterilizer.

Slice the fillets into pieces which will sit nicely in the jars but not sit above the maximum limit. Pour olive oil to cover the tuna completely. Wait for 20 minutes and top up the olive oil (this can also be done more thoroughly by leaving them overnight in the fridge and topping them up the next day).

Screw the tops onto the jars, making sure there is no oil on the rims of the jars and they are completely clean, then place them in the large pot with a teacloth at the bottom to prevent them from rattling too much and cracking. Cover in cold water and bring to a simmer. Simmer gently for two hours and then leave to cool overnight.

The next day, bring to the boil again and simmer for a further 30 minutes. Leave to cool.

Once completely cool, remove the jars from the water and store in a larder on your shelf for years. Leaving them to mature for a year is a good idea. Leaving them for at least six months is strongly recommended.

Boiled Eggs,
Roast Chickens

Sally Finnegan lived on the third floor of
a building on the rue de Seine just off the
Boulevard Saint-Germain on Paris' Left Bank.
She had lived there for half a century and was
turning eighty-seven at the end of the week.
As her body weakened, she found it increasingly
difficult to get up and down the stairs and to walk
around the narrow Parisian pavements with her
walking stick and her bad knee. On good days,
she would sit upon her armchair and read while
the sun streamed in the dusty windows upon
her, warming her gently. And on rainy days, she
would do likewise, but listen to the pitter patter
of the rain upon the windowpane and feel its
harsh cold kept out by the glass, wood and brick
around her. Although she was thankful to still
have her eyesight almost intact and her mind
sharper than ever, she sometimes longed for the
company and excitement she had had all those
years ago when, in her twenties, she had escaped
the boredom and severity of Lahinch and come
to find out what life could offer her here on the
banks of the Seine.

Her daughter had come by earlier in the day to inform her that they would be throwing a party for her birthday which was looming closer. Josephine had some of the physical characteristics of her mother when she was young. She was slight and delicate but had not the rural shame that her mother had carried around but stood tall and proud, at all times sure of herself. She had a fashionable Parisian style and worked in an art gallery. Sally, although proud of her daughter's success, found her confidence to be objectionable at times and preferred modesty always. This, at times, put a wedge between the two.

A great feast was to be had apparently, and although Sally ate very little these days, she was asked by her daughter what she might like to eat. After some short consideration she replied that she might like a boiled egg. Josephine, thinking she was being tedious, took no notice of her. She moved on with the conversation and read out a list of names of family members and close friends who had been invited. Sally had been completely serious regarding the egg. She didn't mind what the others ate but she hadn't the appetite for large meals any longer and she loved a soft-boiled egg from a good hen. It was one of the only nice memories she had of childhood in Lahinch when, in the early morning, dark and still wet with dew, her mother would send her to the back garden where the chicken coop was, to take a few fresh eggs, still warm, for the breakfast. Some brown, some whiter, some speckled, big eggs and small eggs, a variety of choice unknown to us now in these days of uniformity. A fresh egg, boiled and topped with salted butter, scooped out and spread on toast was her greatest luxury in those days and, after so many years away, this had not changed, for her at least. Her daughter left her then, promising to come back and tidy the house for the grand dinner.

All this talk of boiled eggs had given Sally a terrible appetite for exactly that, and so off she went to boil some water in a pan.

Her kitchen was small and narrow and full of pots and pans and all sorts of little useful things which hung from shelves and hooks and any other space she could use. She had a simple gas hob which had not been changed in over thirty years. She filled the small pot and set it to boil and turned on the radio. She often listened to the BBC World Service, but they were interviewing a Tory minister who she couldn't stand to listen to, so she immediately turned it off and simply listened to the hissing of the gas flame and the water coming to a boil.

Some minutes passed while she thought of the farmhouse that she had grown up in and being with her mother in the early morning while she heated the Aga stove and boiled the eggs. It was always damp back home, that was the main memory. The damp and rain and constant wetness of everything inside and outside the house. The mornings were usually particularly freezing, apart from some days in summer when you would get a week or two of sun and it would come out bright and early to heat the earth and shine warmly through the single-pane windows onto the tiled kitchen floor. Despite the weather, it was never as dull as Paris, always having more colour as a consequence of all the plants and flowers growing around – mostly wild ones, she remembered, but some planted by her father at her mother's insistence that they have something decent looking about the house.

Her father would tell her that eating an egg each morning for breakfast would put hairs on her chest, which for some reason she aspired to have in those days. There was not always an egg of course, sometimes the hens wouldn't lay for a few days, weeks even. Some would stop altogether and her father would say it was for the pot. Her mother thought this an awful sin to kill the poor creature and boil it for soup, but her father said waste was a bigger sin and often made the soup himself, which everyone agreed was very good.

Very rarely did they ever have a roast chicken, perhaps only at Christmas or Easter. It was thought of as a total waste to roast a bird rather than boil it and get the broth for soup. On top of that to kill a young bird, necessary for a tender roast chicken, a bird that could lay eggs, was rare. Her father would have never heard the likes of it in his day. When they once did, it was because an aunt had come back to visit at Easter time from France where she had been living. To live in France was a strange and exotic thing to them and she had learned to cook as the French do. She made a gratin dauphinois for the roast chicken and everyone thought themselves the most sophisticated family in the country. Six minutes had passed, and she scooped the egg out of the pot and into the awaiting egg cup. She no longer took toast with her egg and simply opened the top by breaking it with the back of her spoon, scooping out the runny yolk straight into her gob.

Sally sat at the table having finished the boiled egg. It was only ten o'clock in the morning. What she would do for the rest of the day she had no idea. The loneliness and boredom of old age sometimes made her extremely sad. She would have liked to go for a walk through the Jardin des Plantes and maybe over to the Right Bank and into a little bar for a glass of beer, but her aging body did not allow for these young person's dreams. She cleared away the plates and washed them thoroughly at the sink. Although her eyesight was good, she sometimes missed things and her daughter told her she was doting when she found plates stacked on the shelf with little bits of yolk still encrusted on them.

Returning to the room, she sat on her armchair and looked out the window towards the skyline. Remembering the roast chicken of her aunt that one Easter, she picked up the phone and rang her daughter.

'Yes dear, I've decided what we should have for dinner. When did you say it was again? My birthday? Oh, okay. Right then, well, see you then.'

RECIPE

Roast Chicken

Ask your butcher to prepare the chicken for roasting. It is important to truss the bird and it is a good skill to learn, which will not take much effort.

Let the chicken come to room temperature and rub it all over with salt and olive oil. Some people like to put a little thyme, savoury, garlic and butter under the skin which I am not opposed to, but I feel it is perhaps unnecessary. Stuffing the cavity with a lemon or some heads of garlic is a nice addition.

You can start the cooking slow and turn up the temperature near the end, but experience has taught me that bunging it in an oven at 200°C and turning it from time to time for one-and-a-half hours makes a beautiful roast chicken.

Most importantly, rest the bird for 15–20 minutes after roasting.

To carve a chicken: take a sharp boning knife and start by removing the legs, careful not to lose the oysters. Do not be afraid of taking the chicken in your hands and turning it on its side. Cut the legs in half at the joint and place on a warm serving plate.

Next remove both breasts by following
the main bone which runs along the middle,
dividing the breasts. Slice the breasts into three
pieces and place upon the warm platter. Make
a little gravy or jus with the cooking juices and
pour it piping hot onto the carved chicken.

Gratin Dauphinois

Peel and thinly slice some floury potatoes and
wash them thoroughly in several changes of
cold water.

Dry the sliced potatoes and put them in a
bowl with some sliced garlic, thyme, salt, black
pepper, nutmeg and pouring cream.

Butter a baking dish and place the mix inside.
Place more butter on top. Bake with the chicken
for the same duration.

Good served with a green salad, dressed
simply with a mustard, shallot, red wine and
olive oil dressing.

A Soft-boiled Egg

Bring a pan of water to the boil, adding a little salt if you like, as the egg is porous. Lower the flame and carefully place the egg in the water.

Assuming the egg is of normal size and at room temperature, cook for five minutes for very runny, six minutes for runny, seven minutes for soft boiled, eight to nine minutes for hard boiled.

Eat immediately or cool down in plenty of cold water as it will continue to cook in the warm shell.

Home for a While

Con fried bacon on a heavy skillet set onto a gas
stove in the kitchen of his small townhouse.
At the kitchen table sat his young son Fiontan.
He was colouring in and drawing on pieces of
paper, bills turned over and used as sketch pads.
The bills, still unpaid, were ignored for another
week. The child's blond hair glistened in the
morning sun streaming into the kitchen from the
large sash window to the back. He had a big
mop of healthy, shiny hair, and big brown eyes.
His father, unshaven and still in his T-shirt, which
he had slept in, had none of the youthfulness
and energy of his son, life had beaten that out of
him. He stared at the handsome young boy as
he waited for the bacon to crisp, listening to its
sound over the top of the morning radio presenter.
He asked him if he would like a glass of orange
juice with his breakfast or some warm milk
perhaps; it was the boy's first day back to school
and he was treating him to a bacon sandwich.
Sometimes, he would cut the boy's sandwiches
into the letters of his initials, FC, Fiontan
Cassidy. He always made him a packed lunch

to take to school with him and always worried
about him going off alone and wondered was
he often lonely in the playground at lunchtime.
Fiontan had not made many friends since
starting school and preferred instead to spend
his time reading or colouring in or drawing.
His teachers had said that he spent most of
his breaktimes sitting alone on the steps
staring down at the village below the school
and seemingly watching the world go by, un-
interested in what the other children were
doing. He nevertheless ate all his lunch every
day and seemed to appreciate his father cutting
his sandwiches into his initials. His father was
out of work and after taking his son to school
would head off to buy the papers and usually
stop in for a quick pint or two and look at the
job advertisements. His wife, Deirdre, was
working in the post office and brought in just
about enough to pay the rent and buy some
groceries, but he was aware that they could not
go on like this. It was beginning to dawn on
him that he would need to go to England to find
some work. His brother, who was in London,
had said there was plenty of work on the sites
out there and that he would have a place to
sleep on his settee until he got himself settled. It
worried him greatly to leave the boy behind; he
believed that he needed a father around and
was worried that he would be lonely and upset
without his da.

The bacon, crisp and brown, was lifted from the pan. At least we still have rashers to grease our pan, he thought to himself. He poured scalding water from the kettle into a teapot and set about making himself a cup. The boy launched into his sandwich. All the boy ever wanted to do was run around exploring on these warm late summer mornings. Now he was dressed in a green uniform and carrying a heavy bag of books on his back to those dull-looking prefab buildings up the top of the hill.

He helped him tie his shoelaces and told him to pack a raincoat into his bag in case it rained on the way home. Then off they went, walking hand in hand, to the top of the lane and up to the school gates, chatting about the world and the nature around them. He was terrified that something would happen to his son walking home. Cars went so fast around those roads and he didn't trust the drivers to look out for children. Barney McGuire had lost his son in an accident a year ago, knocked clean by the bumper of a big Land Rover which was going too fast and didn't see the boy run out after his football. Barney had never been the same since. Once a successful cattle farmer, he would now be seen often going into the pub at eleven o'clock as soon as it opened and sitting there all day, sometimes singing and laughing, sometimes crying by himself or on someone's shoulder.

Con said goodbye to his son at the school gates, told him to enjoy his lunch, be kind to the other children and good for his teachers. Then he told him to be careful coming home and keep off the roads and that when he got back they would cook together. He had planned to make a lamb stew that evening and it would be a great thing for them to do together, washing and peeling the spuds, chopping the onions and patiently waiting for the thing to be finally ready.

He turned and walked away from the gates, a newspaper protruding from the side pocket of his denim jacket. He needed to have a haircut, it was getting longer and bushy. He called in to his wife to say hello and give her a kiss and ask her for the lend of a tenner to get some groceries. A tour of the town to buy the lamb, onions, potatoes and carrots, then it was time to wet the whistle, he was parched. He pushed in through the door of Rodden's bar and nodded to the usual characters.

'A pint of stout please, Charlie.' Then he sat back and read his newspaper. That damned boat to Holyhead, he thought, if only that wasn't threatening over me I'd live the life of a king. 'A bird never flew on one wing, Charlie, another one for the road.' Then off to make the tea and watch his son colouring in and telling him all about his day at school.

RECIPE

Irish Stew

This is the most simple version I know of a lamb stew and so far the best, although I do appreciate completely different approaches. Both Richard Olney and Paul Bocuse praised the Irish stew for its simplicity, Olney saying it was probably the best of all the stews. It is therefore time that it be seen as such in Ireland.

Take a leg of lamb or, preferably, several necks sliced into rounds of around two centimetres thick. Achieving this with lamb neck on the bone will need the help of a butcher with an electric saw and enough lamb necks. Otherwise, you can use a boned leg sliced into pieces.

Peel and slice floury potatoes around one centimetre thick and a very few carrots. Thinly slice plenty of onions. In a large, heavy pot, layer these up beginning first with onions and then potato, lamb and so on until you have around three or four layers of each, seasoning each layer as you go with salt and pepper. Add water half way up the pot and slowly bring to a simmer and cook for around two hours. The broth should just cover the stew and be light and clear.

Waiting

It was night time by now; it had been dark since five or six o'clock. Jean-Francois had been waiting all evening for his dining partner. There was snow outside. It lay thickly all around the Bearn, on the frozen fields, on the trees and hedges and on the acutely slanted roofs of the farmhouses dotted throughout the countryside. Much of the roads lay covered in snow too and he wondered had his partner been delayed or even stuck somewhere out there in the snow. Each year it snowed like this and the quiet country roads and villages became completely silent. No unnecessary work or travel was done. He himself ventured out from time to time with his 2CV and drove it through the barren countryside. Its interior almost frozen, no heating to warm him, just a large leather coat, lined with wool. He never went far, having nowhere to go. When the house felt like a prison, he left to free himself, but soon realised that he had no one to call on and nowhere of interest to visit and returned home, tired and defeated.

He had a fire put down and was sitting by it, still in a pair of overalls and work boots which he had worn while cutting wood earlier in the day. He was small in stature and stout, with a mop of frizzy, curly hair and although a little overweight, he was incredibly strong.

He listened for the door and to the outside. Nothing. The ticking of a clock. Sometimes it drove him insane and he stopped it. A bang of the door. He turned toward it, only the wind, or a ghost. The bloody ghosts were always playing tricks on him in this old house. Yes, he believed in them, he knew them like old friends. He did not know their names but he had ideas, ideas given to him by stories of who had lived in the house before him and what had happened to them. He did not mind the ghosts, for at times they provided a welcome company, but he distrusted them.

The wind blew against the single-paned windows of the kitchen and he stood up and looked outside at the dark, the white blanket of snow, illuminated by the dim light of the moon. Down below the last field he could see a figure moving. A light, perhaps a lantern, moving along the bottom of the field. It was true there was an old path down there but normally people only used it to walk along by the river in summertime, it would be a dangerous and lonely path on a night like this. Perhaps was it someone who wanted to avoid cars on the road?

It was a neighbour out checking their fields, but for what, at this hour, was anyone doing anything reasonable? He imagined it could be his guest, their car broke down and so they were forced to walk the rest. It would be strange, they would have gone to a village and tried to phone ahead for assistance. He sat down on his chair again by the fire and waited. He tried to concentrate on the fire and poked it with an iron from time to time. He checked the clay pot resting beside the fire and replaced the lid. Simmering away nicely was the garbure, soup of the peasants of Bearn, the smell of cabbage and pork, he was getting hungry.

Again he resumed his seated position, watching the ticking clock and wondering whether or not to pour himself another glass of wine. Not another, you will be drunk when they get here, he told himself.

As another hour passed he became more anxious and forgot his promise to himself not to become drunk. He poured glasses of wine to the brim of his tumbler and drank to stave away the anxiety that his guest may not arrive. Wondering to himself if they had simply forgotten or if, as he suspected, had changed their mind and not wanted to visit him.

His overalls, dirty from the day's work, now had a stain of wine on them. Drunkenly, he had spilled some over himself while taking a sip. He dipped bread in the wine and sat contentedly eating it in his chair. It helped kill the hunger.

As he went to the table to cut another piece of bread he saw again the light that he had forgotten about, steady now, in the snow. Going towards the window he peered out into the blackness; clouds covered the moon now, he observed the faint light flickering in the distance. He wasn't afraid of any man, he told himself, come what will, he would put up a fight.

As he thought this he staggered slightly and sat again by the hearth. This time his bread was greased with a spread of lard from the pan. As he ate, his bristled chin became shiny with the fat. He decided to eat alone. He had been alone for a long time now. His brother had left him to live with a woman who had become his wife. His mother had died ten years ago, his father ten years before that. Now he was completely alone. The bastards, he thought, as he went about setting the table, they couldn't even give an old man some company. He set the table with a shallow bowl and spoon and a piece of bread along with the unmarked bottle of red wine and carried over the large clay pot full of soup.

He dunked the bread and bit into it, then, turning to his spoon, dipped it into the liquid and put it to his greasy chin. Then he heard what sounded like a knock on the door. Putting down his spoon, he sighed, bitter that it had taken them this long to finally arrive. He went to the door and opened it. There was no one there. Confused and drunk he went back to his soup and ate two bowls in quick succession, slurping it back and lifting the bowl to his chin to pour it down his gullet. Soon after he crawled into bed and fell asleep.

The next day he awoke to the daylight, the curtains and window shutters having been left wide open. He walked downstairs to boil water, only to remember the figure from last night. Putting on his winter coat and boots, he walked into the yard and out to the fields but nowhere could he see footprints. It may have snowed overnight and they had been covered. Later, after having breakfast, he got dressed and went out to the car to clear the frost off the window and heat the engine. There had been no snow on the car since yesterday. He drove towards the village to buy a newspaper and when he arrived the lady in the shop said there had been a bad accident up the road, someone had been driving through the dark night and skidded off into the frozen river. They had no chance, they died outright, probably not even having the time to drown before their heart gave in. Jean-Francois bid her a good day and returned to his car. He put on the radio, they were talking about the accident, he turned it off. He drove home and heated up the soup, wondering if his friend would come tonight.

RECIPE

Garbure

This is the typical vegetable soup of the Bearn and Pays Basque. The recipe can be altered but it generally consists of beans, pork and cabbage. They tend to cook it for a long time but it is much better a little fresher.

Onions
Garlic
Leeks
Potatoes
Carrots
Kale
Dried white beans
Salted pork or jambon
Lard
Piment d'Espelette

Wash all the vegetables thoroughly and steep the white beans in water overnight. Set the beans to cook in simmering water for a few hours until tender with the pork. Slice the garlic in rounds and fry in the lard. Add the onions, then leeks, then carrots. When the onions are soft you can add the potatoes and pork and some of the cooking liquor from beans.

Next add the kale and once the potatoes are soft, add the beans and a little more water if necessary. The consistency at the end should be of a hardy, rustic soup. Make sure everything is cut small enough to eat with only a spoon.

Serve with bread and red wine.

The Tide, a Bar on a Saturday Afternoon

It wasn't a warm day, but it was one which was rid of rain and cold winds and so a good one to sit outside of O'Connell's bar and watch the heron in the estuary across the road. Sadhbh wore her cardigan and searched for her glasses while she opened up her copy of the *Irish Times* weekend edition. Her glasses, of course, were hanging around her neck where she'd left them. She sipped her pint and glanced lazily at the articles, which she thought of as under-researched and akin to some professional gossip, but she could never shake the habit of reading the papers, it gave her comfort, like her other habit of sipping a pint in the afternoon of a Saturday.

Across the narrow two-laned road she saw the quiet estuary and some moored fishing boats sitting as still as the water. And what may come now, she thought, as she watched the seagulls hunting for something in the sand, or perhaps for discarded fish and chips. She had woken up early that morning, having finally ended her relationship with her barman friend the night before. It had lasted almost a decade. They both

found comfort in each other, respite from the
loneliness they felt in the small town. But
she did not love him, and neither did he love
her. They tolerated each other, and sometimes
they dreamed that they might love each other.
And on most Saturdays she would wake up
in his bed and then make tea and they might
have breakfast together before she left for her
home. She saw a seagull making a descent
upon a picnic table and took another long sip
of her pint, looking back now and again at
the newspaper, pretending to be interested while
she thought of those mornings making love
in his untidy room, rolling cigarettes at the
back door and drinking her tea while it rained
outside. He was a nice man. He could never
equal her intellectually, but he was kinder than
her. She knew that she was harsh and could
be cruel at times, even with him. Sadhbh was
never a woman to suffer fools lightly and she let
him know when he was foolish. He forgave
her that, and treated her with kindness always,
but he could not understand her. For him it was
not important to be smart, but to be kind
to others.

  She was not a particularly good-looking woman;
since her late twenties she had been overweight
and suffered from eczema on her arms. She
was pleased to have someone show interest in
her, let alone a handsome barman from the
pub up the road. She never did ask him what he

found so attractive about her to ask her to stay
behind for a drink with him that first night. She
was always too scared to ask. But now as she
signalled to the girl collecting glasses for another
pint and folded her paper in two in order to
get a better hold on the thing, she felt wildly free.
The last decade was over and a new one only
beginning. She did not believe in that nonsense
anyway, she thought to herself. Decades and
years and tallying up the beginnings and ends of
things like some convenient little chart. No, life
was much more complex than that. What a silly
idea to think that today was a new beginning.
If she had been speaking to someone about this,
she would have let them know what an eejit
they were.

   The tide was going out, she could see the water
disappearing around the boats, they would
be stranded in the muddy sand soon. The tide was
something that could be relied on to come in
and out, it was circular, not like her chaotic
existence. No, her existence was not chaotic, she
only wished it to be so. Her existence was as
predictable as the tide. On Saturdays she sat here
and sipped a pint and read the newspapers.
In the evening she slept with her lover. Not
anymore. She had changed all that now. She would
go home tonight and make a blackberry and
apple pie. It was the end of summer and the
blackberries were out along the hedgerows and
she could take a walk later by the canal and

pick them. It is true that she had imagined a more exciting adventure as her next one, but this would be a start.

Van Morrison came on the radio, she loved that song, *Linden Arden Stole the Highlights.* She downed the rest of the pint and thanked the girl collecting the glasses. Walking down the road she felt a nice hum off the two pints she had drank and a cool breeze which had picked up from the sea. She would make her pie, and then she might take a ferry somewhere. To France perhaps, and have a little holiday, she thought. The idea terrified her. First make the pastry, she told herself.

RECIPE

Apple and Blackberry Pie

Take equal amounts of flour and butter. Chop the butter into cubes and rub it a little into the flour. It is important to work quickly and keep everything as cold as possible. Have ready a jug of freezing cold water and add this gently until the pastry binds together. Place it in the fridge to rest for 30 minutes.

Remove the pastry and roll it out into a rectangle. Fold it over on itself in three folds so as to create layers. Place back in the fridge for another 30 minutes and repeat. After a last rest, you can then roll it out to fit your pie dish, keeping a little for the lid.

Fill the pie with the fruit, half and half, and sprinkle some sugar on top. Use egg wash to seal the lid on and paint the top with more egg wash. Sprinkle with a little sugar and place in the fridge to cool. Bake in a hot oven (around 200°C) for 45 minutes, gradually reducing the temperature if necessary so as not to burn the pastry. It is important that the pastry sets before the temperature is lowered.

Eating Alone

It was a Sunday in Durango. The day was
announced not only by the clanging bells of
the church tower but by the busy chatter and
clatter of glasses and plates on the terraces of
the small bars which lined the plazas and streets
of the town.

Work had stopped for all but the cooks,
barmen, waitresses and potwashers who pulled
glasses of beer, poured wines and ciders, fried,
baked, boiled, cleared, cleaned and set tables.

Richard had come here alone. Inside him had
grown an unbearable angst to leave home and
so he had come here two days ago and now he
had that strange feeling of both anonymity and
being completely conspicuous that one feels in
a strange but small town. He felt the eyes of the
locals upon him in the small bar where he stood
drinking cider and eating a salt cod omelette
sandwich. His red hair and pale skin stood out
against the unblemished, brown-skinned, dark-
haired people standing around him.

He felt relieved to be here. He did not understand
a word of Spanish and had only a handful of

Basque words which he had studied while waiting in the airport in Dublin. This suited him. He did not want to speak. The chit-chat and niceties of Ireland had begun to sicken him. He was no longer interested in the small talk and idle promises of the bars of Belfast and instead longed to be somewhere he understood no one.

The smells from the kitchen relaxed him and the cider helped calm his nervous brain. The warm autumn day in the street was at odds with the wet October days he had come from and he had not yet passed enough time to learn to miss them.

In a corner, young women with their hair held back with bandanas drank small glasses of beer and shared a plate of fried green peppers. Large men stood at the bar with stout glasses of red wine and greasy fingers picking over txistora sausage and dipping bread into its oily bath.

Richard had planned to have lunch and then sleep through the afternoon, perhaps going for a walk later in the evening and finding something for dinner. He had spent the morning drinking and could feel himself needing to sit down and fill his stomach. The cider was repeating on him and he could feel its acid in his belly.

At the bar he spoke with a man boasting a huge belly in broken English about *callos y morros* and was convinced both by the man's enthusiasm and by his conviction to try anything once. When the tripes arrived to his table he sat in silence and gobbled down the sticky morsels with bread and more cider.

The town of Durango was bombed, like Guernica, he was told. Sometimes, the old men with Alzheimer's would remember it when fireworks went off on New Year's Eve. The bombed town still looked nicer than his bombed town, he thought to himself. He did not tell anyone he thought that. Instead he ate silently and wondered did anyone miss him at home and were they all watching the football in the Rock Bar, because he, for now, did not miss them. But later, when he walked the streets alone in the evening, and the town's citizens had retired to their homes to spend Sunday evening with their families and lovers, and the church bells no longer rang out and no clatter of plates or glasses or chatter was heard on the terraces and even the dogs fell into a sleepy silence, he would miss Belfast and the familiar rowdiness of the packed bar and his friends calling for another round and maybe ordering some chips from Aldo's across the road to eat in the snug.

RECIPE

Callos y Morros

This is the most typical preparation of tripes in the Basque country. It means 'tripes and snouts' and is prepared with some calf head to give it its gelatinous quality.

Boil honeycomb tripe for around 20 minutes and then discard the water and bring to a boil again in fresh water with some aromatics. Do the same with the calf's head. You should aim for around one part head to three parts tripe.

Once both are tender, which will take several hours, chop them into small pieces ready for the stew. Keep the liquor from the head.

Cook lots of sliced onions, plenty of garlic and diced cured ham or chorizo for around one hour until very tender. Add the head and tripe and cover with head liquor. To this add pimento chorizero in its puréed form (or simply roasted and peeled red peppers, finely minced), a little tomato conserve, some bay leaves and plenty of smoked paprika. Cook for around an hour to bring it all together.

Better after a night's rest.

Tuilleamh

On school days,
tea was always on the table
And on Saturdays and Sundays
Friends would be welcome,
To come and eat their fill,
And later,
When we were deemed old enough,
To have a drink on the house.
The kitchen alive with familiar voices,
Stranger or neighbour,
You did not mind,
Everyone had a seat at the table.
If the family was small,
There were plenty of brothers and sisters
At meal times
Fighting over the last morsel of stewed beef.
And in later years,
The door remained open,
Signalling to yet more stragglers,
In streets tucked under the hill,
That warm fires, pots of food and bottles of wine,
Could be found for the lonely,
And to your sons,
That home was always there,
Did they so wish to come back.

Acknowledgements

I'd like to thank Frances Armstrong Jones for her initial encouragement in writing this book, her belief in my writing and cooking and her continual work throughout the entire process, without which none of what is on these pages would have come into being.

Peter Doyle, who kindly contributed his art and particular way of seeing the world, which has made this such a colourful book.

And Rachel Roddy, who has been a guiding star to my cooking, an inspiration in writing and an important supporter from the start. Her words are greatly appreciated by this novice writer.

I would also like to thank the team at *Luncheon* whose professionalism has made this into a beautiful and readable book. In particular Sophie, Josefine and Mariana who passed her Sundays at a kitchen table designing the layout with me.

The recipes included in this book are not entirely my own but what I remember from the generous people who I have met and shared a table with at home and on my travels.

In particular Antoine, Miquel, James, Shaun, Inshaf, Manoj, Dominique, Iban, Eneko, Imanol, Ion Mikel, Maria, Joana, Eudald, Arturo, Rónán, Donal, Breige, Lucy, Conor, Jack, Gareth, Conchur, Niall, Fergal, my mother Moya and my brother Jack.

The stories are of course based on vague memories. Stories cannot be realised without the people who inspire them. This book is a memory of all the characters that I have met in my life, and in this age of homogenization being a character is more important than ever.

Two Dozen Eggs was printed at Graphius, Ghent,
Belgium. Cover prepress by Dexter Premedia.
Two Dozen Eggs is typeset using Bembo and
Perpetua by Monotype.

Two Dozen Eggs is printed on Munken Print Cream and Munken
Polar Smooth (by Arctic paper) which are FSC and EU Ecolabel
certified. Munken is an environmentally friendly and ecologically
sound paper produced at Munkedals in Sweden, which is one of
the world's cleanest fine paper mills.

ISBN: 9780993542381

FIRST PUBLISHED 2023

LUNCHEON EDITIONS